Choices

Choices

--*First Edition*--

Copyright 2016
Published by Ron Celano

All Rights Reserved

ISBN – 13:978-1533610867
ISBN - 10:153361086X

Credits:
Graphic Design - Ron Celano

Composition - Ron Celano

Editing – Barb Celano

While the author has made every effort to provide accurate Internet addresses and other contact information at the time of the publication, neither the publisher nor the author assumes any responsibility for errors or for changes that occur after publication. Further, the publisher does not have any control over and does not assume any responsibility for third party web sites or their content.

Acknowledgments

I would like to thank my wife Barbara, who always stands by me and provides encouragement for the projects I pursue. Additionally, I would like to thank all my intellectual friends that are always willing to participate in vigorous debates no matter the subject. Finally, special thanks go out to my 102 year old dad whose experience in life precedes the depression era. Tapping into his wealth of knowledge provided me with an insight to our nation that I otherwise would not have been able to obtain.

Table of Contents

Choices

Dear Reader

Our freedom to make choices is arguably one of the most important subjects to emerge early in the 21st century. Unfortunately, the freedom to make choices in every facet of our lives is deliberately and systematically being limited or taken away. The dynamics and forces in play are ominous and sometimes subtle, but they are there nevertheless. Americans are at risk and it is time to sound the alarm.

As research for *Choices* progressed, it became apparent that the subject matter could easily fill up more pages than a reasonable length book could tolerate. The topics are complex, many are controversial, and getting to the truth is not always easy. It was finally decided to stay away from the most controversial topics and concentrate on the ones that best convey the message. To that end, the chapters are short (just a few pages) and to the point.

Solutions to issues are not offered as the goal is to inform. On the other hand, suggestions are made in conjunction with certain topics. The purpose is to encourage further research and open debate on the issues. Please be aware that statistics are constantly changing and what is quoted may not be up to date. Nevertheless, they should be kept in mind as they are important to the topic being discussed.

As much as I tried to keep partisan politics out of the dialog in an effort to reduce fodder for the critics and the media pundits, it could not always be avoided. To try and balance things out, there is substantial discussion with regard to conservative, liberal, left liberal, right conservative, and secular progressive ideas as they apply to the context of the topics being discussed. This will surely trigger criticism, smearing, and possibly demonizing, but it is expected and ok. I need the publicity. - Sincerely, Ron Celano

Making Informed Choices

"I am a firm believer in the people. If given the truth, they can be depended upon to meet any national crisis. The great point is to bring them the real facts, and beer." - Abraham Lincoln

Being able to make informed choices based on facts, not only defines freedom, it gives American citizens the unconstrained right to pursue life, liberty, and happiness as stated in the Declaration of Independence. It is not about belonging to any particular political party or about any particular person that holds any kind of government office or about any candidates that might be running for an office. It goes far beyond the petty fighting and smearing that goes on among the parties and candidates. There is a much bigger story in play.

It is about the conditions and dynamics currently occurring in the United States that are influencing its citizen's freedom to make logical choices. That is, choices that are going to determine what their everyday lives and futures are going to be like.

It is about a government run by a political establishment that is responsible for passing legislation regarding laws, regulations, trade, appropriations, treaties, and so on. Americans have become upset and confused as to why their government has become so dysfunctional and why it refuses to serve the people. Traditionally, "We the People" are and have been responsible for those that are elected. Therefore, we would like to think that our elected representatives agree upon and support common principles and values. That is, those that coincide with the founding fathers intentions for this nation. Unfortunately, those principles and values have become less unified as the country continues to diversify and polarize. As a result, it has become less and less apparent as to which principles and values remain common and consistent among the American people.

It is about what still holds us together, our Constitution. Not perfect as written, it has been amended 27 times. The last time was on May 7, 1992. However, it is what guides our principles and without it we would have had nothing to base our legislative or judicial processes on. Without it, our choices become cloudy, our laws become dysfunctional, difficult to interpret, and we lose continuity as a nation. Since the end of World War II, it can be argued that the Constitution has been under attack. Interpretation of laws passed by Congress is sometimes conformed to a specific concept by Supreme Court Justices who rule based on political bias that takes precedence over neutral philosophical judgment.

It is about the media that spins and distorts facts and refuses to disclose when it is doing commentary. It is about a media that suckers political candidates into attacking each other during debates rather than allowing them to address the issues, all for the sake of sensationalism and ratings. Doing so confuses and limits choices regarding what Americans believe or don't believe. These practices are a terrible disservice to the American people who expect unbiased reporting. Alas, it does reveal the character of this nation's people when many seem to be more passionate about a candidate's personality rather than learning how they stand on the issues and what each proposes to do to address them. The media are aware of this and they exploit it often because they know they can get away with it.

It is about laws that are not enforced, open borders, freedom of religion, a declining and expensive educational system, divisive politics, sanctuary cities, fiscal irresponsibility, over regulation, broken and unattainable campaign promises, out of control drug trafficking and use, poverty, crime, a broken and expensive health care system, paternalism, declining freedom of speech and Second Amendment rights, and diminished economic and military standing in the world, to name more than a few. Laws and regulations encompassing these issues in some way or other limits or restricts our choices with respect to how we live, work and play.

It is about an education system that spends more per capita than most other nations in the world, yet ranks 14th in education, 2nd in ignorance, and 24th in literacy.[1] Without a good education, the ability for us to choose a course for our lives and families is diminished and questionable.

So, the question is, "Do the American people still have the capability to make choices based on truth and logic?"

Is Choice a Freedom?

"Your choices are your only freedom." -
Lailah Gifty Akita

Choice is defined as, "The opportunity and power to choose between at least two or more possibilities."[1]   The terms "opportunity" and "power" are very important to the meaning. Opportunity, in this context means that the conditions and facts are acceptable to make a choice. Power applies to the ability to carry out a choice. For instance, you may decide to cut the lawn today because the weather is nice and you have the time and you are feeling well enough to do it (opportunity and power).   Unfortunately, those that are given the power to make decisions that affect the masses are more likely to base their decisions on ideology. A Supreme Court Justice may have to make a choice that requires him to rule on a case that requires an interpretation of the Constitution. He has the opportunity and the power to do so whether his choice is based on facts, previous rulings or his ideology.   Since Supreme Court Justices are appointed rather than elected, "We the People" have no choice in these matters.

Nowhere in the Constitution does it give citizens free choice regarding every aspect of their lives. That would be anarchy. Choices are limited by federal, state and local - laws, regulations, and ordinances. On the other hand, the ability to make choices for oneself, family, and others is the essence of freedom. That is, choices for now and the future that are going to have a positive or negative effect on one's health, wealth and future prospects.

Freedom to choose such things as where we live, where we shop, what we buy, what we read, who we speak to (without fear), and where we send our kids to school are all basic in a free society. Being able to be involved in elections and having a choice of people to vote for occurs in a free society. Otherwise, without these choices or the ability to make them, we are not living in freedom. Wherever the freedom to choose is limited, freedom itself is limited. Wherever the freedom to choose is lost, freedom is lost.

The difference between a democratic and a socialist society is that in a democracy there are basically three classes of people; the upper, the middle, and the lower. The largest being the middle class. Where socialism is the rule of society, there is the upper (rich) and the much larger lower (poor) class. The upper class has total control of society leaving the lower class with few choices. In a fair democracy the lower class always has a path to a better life. Choices are open if people desire to improve their lifestyles. Unfortunately, in this country, at this time in history, the path to a better life for the lower class seems to have disappeared. The Federal Government's irresponsible monetary and fiscal policies along with over regulation and the total disregard for the "good of the people" have virtually made it impossible for the lower class to succeed. Most multi-generation lower class families have given up and no longer believe that opportunities for attaining life, liberty and happiness still exist. The result is that they have little choice regarding how they conduct their lives.

How Choices are Manipulated and Restricted

"Belief can be manipulated. Only knowledge is dangerous." - Frank Herbert

American citizens would like to believe that the choices they make are free choices based on facts. Nothing could be further from the truth. Excluding simple everyday choices, the reference is with regards to more important choices like where we live, work, how we care for our families, and how we vote.

For instance, when The Patient Protection and Affordable Care Act was passed, people no longer had a choice regarding whether they wanted to buy health insurance. That choice was taken away. It was replaced with the choice to either buy health insurance or pay a fine. Furthermore, choices became limited with regard to where and how health insurance is purchased. Consequently, people must go to the "market place" to apply for insurance during the open enrollment period. This is an unpopular and confusing process for many. In fact, the Institute of Business and Technology reports that as many as two million people may have overpaid for their health insurance.[1] This is a case where the choices were so many and so confusing that many people may not have made the best choice for themselves.

Over the last few years the Federal Government (along with many other governments around the world) has been studying and using behavioral science to push people toward a certain outcome in the choices they make. This process is called "nudging." It is really nothing new. After all, companies have been running commercials on TV and ads in newspapers and magazines for years, nudging people to buy their products. Nudging attempts to serve three purposes. First, to dictate our thoughts. Second, to direct our feelings. Third, to control our actions. For instance, people are often nudged to buy an extended warranty when purchasing a product. People are nudged to buy a Part D drug plan when going on Medicare or pay a 10% penalty for drugs (if they sign up at a later date). In the early 2000s, many potential homeowners were nudged to take out mortgages they could not afford. This eventually resulted in a mortgage meltdown that almost destroyed the economy.

The government believes that it should nudge us into making better choices for ourselves and family. In many instances this may be seen as good for us, such as when we are nudged to pay our taxes on time or nudged to go for an annual physical checkup. On the other hand, some believe it is unethical and could be used as a way to manipulate and undermine our choices. For instance, when those choices involve unpopular government ideologies or media agendas. Nudging does not force anyone into a decision, but the practice can be used to distort the facts thus manipulating people into making choices that are not necessarily the best for them. The media are notorious for such practices, especially during elections. Since the media answers to no one and is protected under the first amendment of the Constitution, they can get away with it.

Does the government have the right to manipulate us into making certain choices? Apparently it thinks so. It believes that when our choices may not be clear with regard to health and financial wellbeing, it not only has the right, but the obligation to do so. Although intentional misuse of this tactic by the government is very rare, it certainly seems possible that it could become common practice considering everything else that is going on to limit and restrict the choices we make. Interestingly, there have been cases of bad nudging by the government. For instance, a few years back the Social Security Administration, in an effort to help prospective beneficiaries figure out when delaying claims would offset total benefits, mistakenly placed extra emphasis on the option of claiming early. The result was that early claiming accelerated by 15 months (something the government does not encourage).

There is no "neutral" world in which we make our decisions and choices freely and rationally. Our decisions are constantly influenced, manipulated and restricted by outside forces. That being said, it is more important than ever before to stay vigilant and to try (as hard as it may be) to get to the truth before making any important family or lifestyle decisions.

The Story of a Nation

"To keep any great nation up to a high standard of civilization there must be enough superior characters to hold the balance of power, but the very moment the balance of power gets into the hands of second-rate men and women, a decline of that nation is inevitable." - Christian D. Larson

Parts of the following text are paraphrased from a video by Jerry Rye, that at the time of this writing was circulating around the Internet.[1] Although a true story, the author cannot attest to the complete truth of the content, but if desired it can be researched and verified. Actually, it does not really matter. It is the conclusion of the story that is important, including the events that lead up to such.

Early in the 1900s a country existed that was one of the richest countries in the world. While Great Britain's empire was unsurpassed with its naval power, only one other nation (which will be revealed shortly) challenged this country for the position of the world's most powerful economy.

This country had abundant agriculture with

expansive, rich farmlands that were accessible through navigable waterways and extensive ports. It's railroads, automobiles, telephones, and level of industrialization was higher than a lot of European countries.

Eventually, for reasons that were thought noble at the time, the people elected a new president that promoted "Fundamental Change." That is, changes that appealed to both the middle and lower classes. Some programs that were implemented to stimulate the economy included mandatory pension insurance, mandatory health insurance, and funding for low-income housing construction. Simply put, the government assumed economic control of a large majority of the country's previous public operations. It then began assessing new taxes to fund its takeovers. Choices for the people started to decline as mandatory programs were put into place.

The entitlement programs grew, boosted by the increased flow of revenue. In time, the government payouts became overly generous and its outlays surpassed the value of taxpayer contributions. When that happened the entitlements became underfunded and the economy began to stress.

Large scale economic suffering eventually resulted in the election of a corporatist president (a person that believes in corporatism or corportavism - the sociopolitical organization of a society by major interest groups, or corporate groups, such as agricultural, business, ethnic, labor, military, patronage, or scientific affiliations, on the basis of common interests).[2] His charismatic wife supported his populist rhetoric to continue taxing the rich. Eventually, increased taxes were expanded to cover most of the middle class. Choices became more and more limited as people's lives were constrained by less income and other strangulation policies.

Under the new president, the size of government bureaucracies continued to grow through massive programs of social spending. The growth of labor unions was encouraged. These programs provided government jobs that attracted the farmers and cattlemen. They had no other choice because they could no longer make a living on their individual farms and ranches. They could no longer compete with the large corporate groups. This led to reductions of beef and wheat because these commodities were controlled by the corporate groups who mismanaged production.

Eventually, the president was driven from office, but not before high taxes and economic mismanagement took their inevitable toll. However, his contempt for economic realities and populist rhetoric remained popular. The government continued to build up its debt by spending far beyond its means.

Does any of this sound familiar to you? If you are thinking that this is what is happening right now in the United States of America you would be correct, but the country described is not the United States. The United States is the country that this country was second to in the size of its economy. It is the story of Argentina and what follows next are extraordinary lessons regarding government bureaucracies, controls, inefficiencies, waste, and corruption.

Since the Argentina's monetary system was based on another nation's currency, its currency was not allowed to fluctuate according to supply and demand. By the 1970s, inflation was so bad that taxi cab drivers had to adjust their meter readings daily to keep pace. Insufficient beef led to meatless days because not enough beef was grown to satisfy the local markets. This was in a country that had exported beef for many years. Formerly one of the major wheat exporters of the world, it had to start importing wheat to satisfy demand.

Hyperinflation took hold late in the 1980s as things grew worse. Industrial protectionism, redistribution of income based on increased wages and growing state intervention in the economy persisted.

The economy continued to decline as the government added (printed) more money to pay off its public debts. Inflation hit 3000% reminiscent of Germany between 1919 and 1933. Riots were rampant as starving people looted stores and the country descended into chaos.

By 1994, Argentina's public pensions – the equivalent of Social Security – were broke and were no longer able to be sustained. Payroll taxes had increased from 5% to 26%, but revenue still fell short. In addition, a value-added tax (VAT) was implemented (today it runs from 10.5% to 27% and is charged on practically all goods, services and investments).[3] In addition, new income taxes, a personal tax on wealth, and more revenues based upon the sale of public enterprises crushed the private sector and further damaged the economy. In 2001 the government replaced those funds with its defaulted bonds.

Eventually, government fiscal irresponsibility led to a national economic crisis that was equivalent to the American "Great Depression." The government was driven from office once again as austerity policies combined with the loss of confidence in the financial system led to large scale protests. Default on the country's external debt followed and in January 2002 the convertibility regime was formally abandoned. The choices that remained for the populace were limited to their daily struggles.

Early in the 20th century Argentina was one of the richest countries in the world. With the great socialist experiment over, it had been reduced to a poverty-stricken country that struggled to meet its debt obligations amidst continued economic problems.

Today, Argentina is making slow progress towards a recovery. Many of its fiscal policies are still in question, but it seems to be learning from the lessons of the past. Unfortunately, the country had to go through years of struggles that included many military coups.

During Argentina's history of the last century, there were many warning signs of what was to come. At what point people lost control of their country is debatable. It could be argued that it happened when they lost their choices.

History is abundant with failed socialist experiments. Socialism always seems to end up the same way. That is, with countries destroyed and their peoples devastated. Today, we see the same thing happening in Venezuela[4] and in other countries around the world.[5]

At this time, the same warning signs are present in the United States of America (keep them in mind as you read on). Some would say we are just a few years away from what happened in Argentina. It is yet to be seen whether people are still vigilant and able enough to avoid the crisis that surely will come if things continue in the same way. Will we heed the lessons of Argentina and other failed socialist nations? Choices for Americans are becoming more limited every day. Let's hope we solve our issues before they run out.

The First and Second Amendments to the Constitution

"The strength of the Constitution lies entirely in the determination of each citizen to defend it. Only if every single citizen feels duty bound to do his share in this defense are the constitutional rights secure." - Albert Einstein

Nothing seems to conjure up more discussion or is under attack more now-a-days then the first two amendments to the Constitution. Let's take a look at each and see how they protect our freedom to make choices in regard to them.

The First Amendment states that:

> Congress shall make no law respecting an establishment of religion, or prohibiting the free exercise thereof; or abridging the freedom of speech, or of the press: or the right of the people peaceably to assemble and to petition the Government for redress of grievances.

Adopted a little over four years after the signing of the Constitution, these few words say a lot. First, they prevent the government from establishing a national church/denomination. In other words, state-sponsored religion is forbidden. However, they do not prohibit God from being acknowledged in schools, government buildings, on our currency, or in our Pledge of Allegiance to the flag as the secular progressives would like us to believe. Although the government cannot establish a church or religion, those first words do not guarantee the separation of church and state. Could a church and the state become one? Not likely, but it would be possible if a group like the Islamic State were to gain control of the government. No more needs to be said.

Although there is often extreme intolerance between religious groups, the First Amendment gives all American citizens the choice as to what religion they wish to follow as long as they abide by the laws of the country. It does not give any religion the right or power to remove all the vestiges of another faith from the public. Unfortunately, we are seeing this very thing happen on a more frequent basis today. You've heard or read about or may have firsthand experience with secular progressives or religious groups that try to stop holiday greetings or stop people from putting up a Christmas tree or a nativity scene on private or public property. There was actually an attempt to stop an Easter egg hunt in a prominent Midwestern city because the flyers that were passed out upset parents and children of a certain religious group.[1]

Freedom of speech and the press are guaranteed under the First Amendment, but both under attack. Suppression of freedom of speech is rarely carried out by the government. It is usually carried out by left wing tyrants that refuse to hear the opposing view for fear that they will be challenged and will have no rebuttal. Nowhere is this more apparent than in the nation's educational system. More on this is covered in a later chapter.

The press (and other types of media) takes what is happening in the educational system even further. Freedom of the press was included as part of the First Amendment because it was believed that the press would inform the people by exposing questionable actions and policies of our leaders. Today, just the opposite is happening as many media outlets align themselves with one particular ideology or another. The result is that the American people rarely hear the complete truth.

The right to peaceful assembly and protest has been used successfully many times throughout history to show dissatisfaction with the actions of local, state and the Federal Government. However, that right does not give people or groups the right to assemble for the purpose of creating mayhem, destroying property, inciting riots, threatening people, blocking traffic, and disrupting private events - all of which we are seeing on a more frequent basis today. Although there are laws that are supposed to prevent such chaos from happening, authorities seem to be more and more powerless to do anything about it as they are afraid to offend anyone or any group. As lawlessness grows, tougher laws and tactics to suppress such will surely ensue. As a result, our choice to assemble freely could become severely limited.

The Second Amendment states that:

A well-regulated Militia, being necessary to the security of a free state, the right of the people to keep and bear Arms, shall not be infringed.

Well over 200 years since the Second Amendment was added to the Constitution, the debate still rages on over whether it recognizes the right of each citizen to keep and bear arms or whether the right belongs solely to state governments, empowering them to maintain a military force (National Guard). As the debate continues, the fact remains that citizens are still able to keep and bear arms. Citizens currently have the choice to own a gun or not own a gun. This precedence has been set since December 1791.

Originally, it was believed that citizens should have guns in case of invasion as the populace would be able to assist the military. That is an impracticable argument today as guns would have no effect on a war fought in the nuclear and technology age. Another argument is that allowing citizens to own guns will allow them to discourage or thwart off a tyrannical government that may have ideas of taking over the country by force. Again impracticable, as a tyrannical government would surely have weapons that totally "out gun" any weapon(s) that ordinary citizens might own. The caveat here is that history has shown over and over again that when guns are taken away it opens the way for a tyrannical government takeover. Lastly, some believe that citizens should own guns for self-protection, especially since acts of terrorism are on the rise. Of the three arguments the last seems the most logical and reasonable.

Gun control advocates say that crimes committed with guns can be reduced by restricting or eliminating guns all together. Several laws, regulations, and executive orders have already been passed that advances their cause. For instance, it is against the law to own automatic weapons and has been since 1986. Background checks are required when buying most guns. (Guns made before a certain year are exempt.) These and other restrictions seem to be good ideas, but if the current trend continues, there is a danger that the Second Amendment could be eventually rendered useless. For instance, laws could be established that say guns can only be made out of mashed potatoes and can only shoot bullets made from butter. In this scenario citizens would still be able to own guns, but obviously they would be useless as a means of defense. Sounds ridiculous, but the example illustrates the point.

Since this book is about choices, it will not get into the merits or unworthiness of owning guns. There are countries that have totally banned guns and others that require all their citizens have guns. Ultimately, the American people will decide, through their elected leaders, whether guns should be allowed, how much they are restricted, or if they should be eliminated. No matter if you are for or against guns, in the end it comes down to whether or not you want to give up another choice.

One of the great things about the Constitution, and one that few people think about, is that it was intentionally written in such a way as to promote open debate among the people. Therefore, laws and regulations should represent the will of the people. Of course, it was assumed that the American people would be able to do so based on facts and the truth.

Political Correctness

"Political correctness is modern day censorship. This still doesn't justify you in being a douche bag." - Kevin Focke

Political correctness (PC) and honest communication (HC) are on two ends of the political dialog with propaganda smack dab in the middle (PC<<<<<propaganda<<<<<HC). Politicians, the media, and academia would like us to believe that political correctness is about politeness or being respectful, sensitive and caring or avoiding hurt feelings or manners. But, shouldn't we be striving to do those things anyway without anyone telling us to do so? If it is not the above, then what exactly is it? It is best described as the use of propaganda to manipulate the way people speak, write, think, feel, and act to further an agenda.

Like all propaganda, it is about avoiding the truth by altering reality. Simply put, PC is a lie that refuses to deal with the underlying nature of reality. Politicians are masters at PC, promising easy solutions while avoiding tough discussions. That is, honest discussions that are needed to solve our biggest problems. Unfortunately, a culture of honesty, diversity, and respect has no place where the legal and elite practice a certain speech code that precludes discussion of tough issues.

When it comes to PC, anything goes. The following illustrates some outrageous examples of PC at work:

San Francisco libraries have installed small plastic "privacy screens" on their computers. These were installed so that perverts could continue to watch pornography without exposing children.[1]

A school in North Carolina ordered a six-year-old girl to remove the word "God" from a poem that she was supposed to read during a Veteran's Day ceremony.[2]

A student at Florida Atlantic University was suspended from class for refusing to write "Jesus" on a piece of paper, put it on the floor and stomp on it.[3]

There are thousands of incidents like these that are being carried out all over the country. In addition, there are certain words and phrases that are now taboo. Here are just a few: pet owner - transformed into "pet guardian;" Christmas - transformed into "happy holidays;" prayer - transformed into "thoughts;" global warming - transformed into "climate change," and the best one of all: terrorists transformed into "misguided criminals." In addition to words, correct grammar may be deemed offensive. When a UCLA professor corrected some spelling and grammar errors found in student papers, he was accused of microagression against the students.[4]

It should be understood that the purveyors of PC are not asking for your opinion and they certainly are not inclined to debate you. Their agenda is to divide us, by class, race, sex, and sexuality so that we comport with their sense of social justice.

Aside from the obvious, every single day those of authority and in the public eye such as the mainstream media, politicians, and academia try to indoctrinate us with subtle messages about what we should believe and what is appropriate. That is, how we should act and speak. Be on the lookout for PC and you will soon come to recognize it. You will realize that PC intends to rob us of our independence of thought. You will then understand that it is about control that limits or takes away our freedom to make choices as it molds and remakes us into something not based on logic, but rather on ideological nonsense.

The Media

"Whoever controls the media, controls the mind" - Jim Morrison

Since the Bill of Rights was signed in 1791, there has been much debate over the meaning of "Congress shall make no law...abridging the freedom of...the press". UCLA law professor Eugene Volokh attempted to clarify the issue in his 2011 article, *"*The Freedom of...the Press, From 1791 to 1868 to Now - Freedom of the Press as an Industry, or the Press as a Technology," by stating that, "...the founders really meant something more like "freedom of...the printing press" or "freedom in the use of the press.?""[1] In this context, freedom of the press means the right of free men to write, print, or publish, his or her thoughts. Of course before modern day media, the means to do so was with the use of a printing press.

Today's communication technologies include TV, radio, print, and the Internet. Collectively, these technologies are commonly referred to as "the media." For our purposes, it is not the way the media is delivered, that we are interested in. It is the media heads, journalists, and others that align themselves with certain ideologies and then use the media to distort facts and spread their dogma. Some of this may be due to the fact that sometimes there are family ties between the media and our elected leaders.[2] Unfortunately, there is nothing in the Constitution that says that the press/media must remain neutral or honest in their reporting.

Although there are laws protecting citizens from defamation (libel and slander), the laws do not necessarily protect us from distorted facts. Additionally, laws that require media journalists to distinguish between factual news and commentary (opinion) or deception (except in advertising) are either weak or do not exist. A 2013 Pew Research Center study found that as much as 85% of programming at news stations is commentary.[3] The once-clear line between opinion and news, drawn to separate editorial viewpoints from daily coverage, has all but disappeared. That line separated the personal view of the media heads and journalist from the news reported to the public.

The rise in partisan voices in public forums has been on the rise in the last couple decades as they slant current affairs and other news to reflect their own agendas. Today, nothing is off limits. The blurring of news and opinion handicaps public understanding of current affairs, candidates position on issues, and how to solve them, including pending legislation in Washington.

Opinions aside, deception or the use of trickery and psychological manipulation to create a desired action upon the people is often used to serve ideological purposes. In the political world, the word "spin" is substituted for deception as it is a politically correct, polite description. It is used by the media, businesses, political leaders, lobbyists, and political parties alike to shape events and to make someone or something look better (or worse) than anybody or anything else. Spin is used to mislead the public by bending facts, using subtle omissions, misquoting or ignoring the words of others, painting false pictures, and sometimes resorting to outright lies.

It usually goes something like this: - A political candidate says that she is against illegal immigration and the news media reports that she is against immigration (leaving out illegal), making it sound like she is against all immigration. Next, so called "experts" are introduced to provide analysis of the candidates' comments. Since the analysts' views are ideologically the same as the media, they resort to delegitimizing and demonizing tactics. Unfortunately, many people still trust and believe what they hear from the media, not realizing that they are being deceived. This practice can no better be illustrated than in a statement by Richard Salent (1914-1994), former president of CBS News. He stated, "Our job is to give people not what they want, but what we decide they ought to have."[4]

With the advent of the Internet, social media websites such as Facebook, Twitter and others began to appear. What better way to spread deception, then to use these tools to influence the public, especially when they are near impossible to regulate or officiate. After all, friends and followers are more likely to read and pass on information they receive from somebody they know. This all happens at lightning speed. If the post goes "viral," it could virtually reach millions of people in America or around the globe within a few hours.

Whenever an opinion or a deception is posted on Facebook, Twitter, or any other social media site, it is propaganda designed to make those who read it, think about an issue or behave in a certain way that contributes to the viewpoint of the author. In today's fast paced get it done yesterday world, people do not have the time or the desire to get to the truth, so the deception is passed on.

The continued and constant use of such tactics and tools deceive millions of people every day. Blurring of facts with opinion and the use of deception makes it nearly impossible for anyone to make a logical choice based on facts. The result is a lost choice that has cleverly and deliberately been taken away.

Education

"The aim of public education is not to fill the young of the species with knowledge and awaken their intelligence. Nothing could be further from the truth. The aim is simply to reduce as many individuals as possible to the same safe level, to breed and train a standardized citizenry, to put down dissent and originality. That is its aim in the United States." - Henry Mencken, *The American Mercury,* April 1924

It is interesting that Henry Mencken ("...regarded as one of the most influential American writers and prose stylists of the first half of the twentieth century" - Wikipedia) recognized what was going on within our education system way back in 1924. The "dumbing" down of America continues today as verified in the 2015 National Assessment of Educational Progress report, also known as "The Nation's Report Card."[1] It states that, "When it comes to reading and math skills, just 34 percent and 33 percent, respectively, of U.S. eighth-grade students tested proficient or above."

When it comes to young adults in high school, it doesn't get any better. The 2010 and 2013 NAEP test scores show that only 38 percent of 12th-graders were proficient in reading, 26 percent were proficient in math, 12 percent in history, 20 percent in geography, and 24 percent in civics. Yet, many of these poorly performing students will gain entry into a college (astounding!).

A country that spends more per capita on education than most other nations in the world, yet ranks 24th is a shameful commentary. It would seem that the issue is not about money. Yet, many inner city and other school precincts are sorely in need of funds. Buildings in disrepair, shortages of supplies and books, inadequate oversight, and out of control students (with more and more resorting to violence) are common problems. Some blame can be attributed to declining neighborhoods where property tax revenues don't provide enough funds to keep up.[2] Mismanagement of funds, fraud, corruption and insufficient oversight can also be blamed. In addition, broken down family values and structure contributes to the disrespect and violence. Political forces fighting to gain an advantage in state precincts magnify the issue. The result is that money is not distributed equitably among all school districts.

Aside from money, a large part of the problem is that students are taught more about social justice, environmentalism, sex, and less about important subjects such as American history, English grammar, math, literature, music, and art. Textbooks are or have been rewritten to portray America as an immoral nation characterized by colonialism, racism, economic exploitation, militarism, and other apologetic subjects.[3] These same textbooks conveniently leave out the facts that America has been the beacon of freedom to mankind, the country that has spent more money and spilled more blood to liberate other people than any other nation.

Common core standards stand at the center of these issues. This is a case where big government interference has created a disaster by de-funding and over regulating. This is a much larger subject than can be covered in this book, but more information can be found here.[4]

Some believe that much of what is happening within the educational system is to advance left liberal ideas. That is, liberal ideas that have their roots in the social movements of the 1960s. Liberal institutions, afraid that students, teachers and professors will be exposed to an alternative way of thinking (especially at the college level), often intimidate those into silence. Kirsten Powers sums it up this way in her book, *The Silencing*, "When people are afraid to express their opinions because they've seen other people treated as deviants deserving of public shaming or worse, they will be less likely to speak freely."[5]

There have been many instances where speakers were not invited or were uninvited to speak at college commencements because they had views opposing those of the college or student body. A 2014 article in U.S. News and World Report stated, "Conservatives are disappearing from commencement programs, according to Harry Enten at the data-crunching site FiveThirtyEight. "Over the past two years, the top 30 universities and top 30 liberal arts colleges hosted 20 political commencement speakers, with nary a conservative in their ranks. Quite a change from 10 years earlier, when political speakers were more evenly split between liberals and conservatives."[6] In many instances speakers are screened and must agree to certain conditions. If they do get to speak, they are often interrupted, sometimes to the point of being shouted off the podium. In 2016, Michael Bloomberg (former mayor of New York City) was soundly booed at a University of Michigan commencement when he blasted the idea of "safe spaces" and other coddling of college students by college administrations.[7]

Although most colleges promote free speech, there are many examples where it is restricted. For instance, many colleges restrict free speech to what are called "free speech zones" that limit activity to a patch of grass, gazebo, or a few square feet on a patio. Despite rulings by federal judges that free speech zones are unconstitutional, FIRE (Foundation for Individual Rights in Education) indicates that about 1 in 6 of the top colleges in the country still have them.[8]

Some universities are demanding that Christian groups adhere to policies that go against Christian values and beliefs or they will be de-recognized.[9] This creates a stigma for such groups and the message that they should be avoided.

The lack of free speech and secular policies in the

American education system are setting a dangerous precedent. Are the left liberals winning? Where else to make a large impact on a country's future than through its education system? How are young people going to make informed choices regarding freedom and democracy when they are brought up and educated to align themselves with the far left, while at the same time being shielded from opposing points of view? Yes, it does seem that the left liberals are winning, as we see our younger generations falling in line to support socialist agendas. This is no more apparent than in the 2016 presidential primary elections.

Some of these young adults will invariably end up in the political mainstream and some will most likely be elected to Congress. Imagine a Congress where opposing views are routinely censored by shouting and other types of disruptions.

The cost of education at the university level has quadrupled over the last 30 years. Today student loan debt stands at over a staggering $1 trillion, more than the credit card debt of every American combined.[10] According to the College Board, the average cost of tuition and fees for the 2015–2016 school year is $32,405 at private colleges, $9,410 for state residents at public colleges, and $23,893 for out-of-state residents attending public universities.[11] Of course, tuition at the elite colleges such as Harvard and Yale is much higher.

Many believe that the Federal Government is to blame for the current rise. In 2010, legislation was passed ending subsidies for private banks that offered federally guaranteed student loans. The result was that the Federal Government, not banks, became the lender of choice for most students. Is it a coincidence that the more money the Federal Government pumps into financial student aid, the more money the colleges charge for tuition? Some say it is not a coincidence and that tuition's are artificially high directly because of federal financial aid. On top of it all, students are solely responsible for paying back loans, since loans are no longer "dis-chargeable," or covered by bankruptcy. Choices for young adults that want to go to college are becoming more limited every year. It is either burden themselves with a huge debt or try to make a living without a college education. When the thought of incurring a high debt stands in the way of getting a higher level of education, it is not hard to understand why people stuck in low paying jobs want higher minimum wages.

Jobs and Wages

"Big jobs usually go to the men who prove their ability to outgrow small ones." Ralph Waldo Emerson

Fifty or so years ago young adults were able to earn money by working a variety of part time jobs while they were in junior or high school. In rural areas they worked on farms. In the cities and the suburbs, they cut lawns, delivered papers, babysat, worked at their fathers or grandparents' business, and so on. They understood the responsibility that came with hard work. They learned the value of money and knew early on that success in life required a college education or some other formal training after high school. It wasn't easy for everybody as there was crime, drug and alcohol related problems in many areas of the country. That being said, those issues were not nearly the problem that they are today. Those that worked part time, usually continued to do so when they went to college and most graduated with little or no debt.

A four year degree just about guaranteed a good job. There was also an abundance of good jobs for those that received a two year degree. If college was not an option, then there were trade schools and other training programs available. Although not the most desirable, relatively good paying jobs were also available for those that did not go to college. In fact, in 1960 about 1 in 4 people had manufacturing jobs, most of which were learned on the job. Today, the number is less than 1 in 10 and most require some sort of high-tech training or at least a two year college degree.[1]

The culture has changed considerably since then. In many cities across the country, children and young adults gravitate to the streets getting caught up in the drug and gang cultures. They find it easier and more profitable to make money selling drugs than to work for it. In the more affluent areas, many parents are over protective, giving their children large allowances so they don't have or want to work. They make sure their children are involved in as many activities as possible. The belief being that these things will protect them from bad outside influences. This is understandable, but the result is that the work ethic and learned values of the past have all but disappeared.

Today, most of the part time jobs are taken by adults that are trying to make ends meet as they have few other choices. Full time jobs are sometimes hard to come by for a variety of reasons. Many job losses can be attributed to automation while others have disappeared because a growing number of companies are shipping jobs out of the country or have opted to build plants in other countries. This is always a political hot topic as many blame bad free trade agreements with foreign countries. On the other hand, it could be surmised that if not enough jobs exist in a country, then something is wrong in the country failing to produce those jobs. Businesses that are overly hampered by government regulations, taxes, and other impairments are not going to be as economically vibrant as they might be otherwise.

Interestingly, there are a growing number of high tech jobs, and jobs in other sectors that are not being filled. Steve Langerud of Steve Langerud and Associates, LLC states, "Firms know how real it is. They see how much money it costs them by having to pay a premium for talent, and they see the money lost in services they cannot provide to clients because they don't have workers."[2]

Terry Howerton, managing partner of TechNexus states, "The long-term scarcity springs from a deficient educational system."[3] Obviously, there is disparity between the number of jobs available and the people being educated or trained for those jobs. Higher level education that costs too much and promotes liberal political orthodoxy over education and academic freedom is not going to solve the issue. Without affordable education targeted toward job markets that need workers, people have no choice but to seek work in the lower paying full and part time job sectors.

According to the Economic Policy Institute, wages have been stagnant for the last 35 years.[4] They also suggest that any increase in wages has been chewed up by inflation. Since the government does not include food and energy in its calculations, it is probably a lot worse than meets the eye. In fact, the income divide between the upper, middle and lower classes continues to grow. There are a number of reasons for this and it is not solely the fault of the rich as the left liberals would have you believe. A large part of it is because of the education gap, since it affects both wages and net worth.

The future for higher wages doesn't look any brighter. According to a 2014 study done by the U.S. Conference of Mayors and IHS Global Insight, new job positions have pay levels that are 23% lower than the jobs that have disappeared. The study further states that in many cases, low-wage and often part-time jobs are replacing high-wage full-time jobs in sectors like technology, manufacturing and construction. J.P. Morgan Chase along with the Congressional Budget Office predicts that gross national product growth is going to be a dismal 1.25 percent through the year 2017.

Until conditions are changed so that companies can compete in this country and until people wake up to what is going on in the education system (and has it corrected), those seeking work will have little choice but to find it where they can and take the wages that are offered to them.

Poverty

"If the misery of the poor be caused not by the laws of nature, but by our institutions, great is our sin." - Charles Darwin, *Voyage of the Beagle*

The 2015 Census Bureau report puts the official poverty rate in America at 14.8%, which equates to around 46.7 million people.[1]   The median income of a family of four that is considered in poverty, is $24,250 a year or $466 a week or about $12.00 an hour - calculated over a 52 week period. Most of the people in poverty that work receive some kind of government assistance. The U.S. has one of the highest levels of per capita government social-welfare spending among affluent nations. In fact, just one nation (Norway) spends more per person than the U.S. does.[2]

Welfare in itself sounds like an all-inclusive term. In actuality, there are many welfare programs. They provide everything from cash, food, housing, medical care, and social services to poverty stricken Americans. Total spending on these programs now reaches over $1 trillion annually.[3]

Survey after survey shows that people would rather be self-sufficient, other than on welfare. If they had the choice, they would like to have good jobs that provide a path to better wages and benefits. They would like to be able to send their kids to good schools and they would like to live the much hyped American dream. That being said, most people that are at or below poverty take advantage of welfare programs that in some cases provide benefits way above the stated poverty level. For example, a controversial 2013 Cato Institute study reports that welfare benefits sometimes pay much more than a minimum wage job in 33 states.[4] Thirteen of those states pays the equivalent of more than $15 per hour ($28,800 annually). The most generous benefit package is in Hawaii, which pays $49,910 annually. People that take advantage of most, if not all, available welfare benefits (especially in states like Hawaii), are more likely to choose to stay on welfare because their total income is sufficient to live on.

The Clinton Welfare-to-Work program, passed in 1996, requires most people to work (within a certain time period) in order to get welfare benefits.[5] At that time, anti-poverty programs were shifted from the Federal Government to the states which were required to implement new models of welfare as they saw fit. So, what happened? Do those in poverty today have more or better choices that are going to lead them towards a better lifestyle?

One thing for sure, being in poverty is not a simple life as alternative means aren't a choice for those who are stuck in poverty. Coping and adjusting from day to day takes its mental as well as physical toll. In addition, not all people in poverty can take advantage of the high paying benefit packages that are offered in some states. We already learned why the education system is not helping matters. We also learned why the job situation is not helping either. Legislation like the Patriot Act also doesn't help as a growing number of establishments now require credit cards over cash, that which someone in poverty is less likely to have. The fact is, the few choices that are left for those in poverty are rapidly disappearing.

To further highlight the poverty dilemma, let's take the example of the desire for higher minimum wages. The federal minimum wage for covered nonexempt employees, at this time, is $7.25 per hour. Since most people that are in poverty don't see better jobs in their future, they choose to push for higher minimum wages. The current mantra is to raise the federal minimum wage to $15.00 an hour. This certainly seems logical, especially to those in poverty. Let's take a closer look. Since small businesses (who provide two thirds of new jobs) run on relatively small profit margins, it is likely that higher minimum wages would lead to less available full time jobs and higher prices for consumers. Some would disagree, but the benefits are questionable as it is likely that there would be a negligible net positive result. Since everyone would have to pay higher prices, lifestyles would drop a notch across the board. The effect would be minimal for most, but this kind of thinking would certainly lead to other income redistribution ideas.

There are better ways to improve and eventually solve the poverty issue, but it will require a change in the way our culture thinks. With the way Americans are divided today, it is not clear whether they can stomach or want to support changing back to the values, hard work, and unabated education that made this country great in the first place. That is, if the job situation is ever to improve. If not, we are going to continue slipping closer and closer to a socialist state where there are just two classes of people, the rich and the poor.

Redistribution of Wealth

"All legislative experiments in the way of making forcible distribution of the wealth produced in any country have failed." - Leland Stanford

The traditional definition of egalitarianism is the belief that all people are equal and deserve equal rights and opportunities. In today's world, that meaning has been skewed to mean that all people are equal (literally) and deserve equal rights and entitlements. Entitlements such as food stamps, Medicaid, social security disability benefits, Earned Income Tax Credit and others are typically paid for by taxing the affluent. This is otherwise known as redistribution of wealth. In addition, other programs such as social security retirement benefits, unemployment benefits, the minimum wage, Medicare, and subsidies for education have a large redistributive component to them.

Spending on entitlement programs was basically negligible until the Great Depression of the 1930s. In fact, it was barely over 0.4% of the Gross Domestic Product (GDP) or about 5% of all government spending.[1] Today, it stands at 21.1% and is expected to grow to 23.1% by 2026.[2] Those numbers do not include state and local spending.

Millions of citizens who are not self-sufficient, for one reason or another, have a vested interest in these benefit programs. They have no choice because they have become victims of the system. They lost control and their choices when they were transformed and transported into a lifelong, low expectation lifestyle by a so called well-meaning Federal Government. They must be kept where they are so that the government can pass more laws in order for millions of government employees to have jobs. Those that have paid into the system (Social Security and Medicare) believe that they are due lifelong benefits after retirement because it is their money. Actually, most will get much more out of these systems than they put into them.

President Ulysses S. Grant talked about how government entitlement programs destroy independence and create a nation of co-dependents. He talked about how they sap our pioneering spirit, and the genius which built our country.[3] He said that they would deplete our Treasury, and turn virtually all of us into useless appendages of the State. We see this happening today as the government raids trust funds, raises the debt ceiling and prints money with abandonment. With no sensible solutions left to ponder, the left liberals call for higher taxes on the rich and look for other ways to steal from American citizens to justify and ensure their existence. We saw what happened earlier when a government, as a last resort, took over control of private pension funds. Don't think that can happen in America? In July 2015, the Independent Sentinel reported that, "High on the socialist dream list is big government control of private savings and retirements."[4] If this happens, we will see more redistribution of wealth, right into the hands of the Federal Government.

A democracy cannot exist as a permanent form of government when the majority has no choice but to vote for the candidate promising the most benefits from the public treasury. The result is always the same. That is, the demise of that democracy.

Free Enterprise

"There's no limit to what free men and free women in a free market with free enterprise can accomplish when people are free to follow their dream." - Jack Kemp

A free market or capitalism is based on a free enterprise system. It is characterized by having different companies competing for your business. This usually leads to lower prices and better or similar quality products. People have the ability to choose and seek employment based on their interest and education or to determine what type of business they want to own. When starting a business, they have the right to determine where it is located, who to buy supplies from, how they want to set prices, and how much profit is acceptable. In a true free market system, supply and demand determine prices and profit. In a socialist system, the central government controls everything.

Lately, you may have heard about how over regulation is stifling small and large businesses alike. The following story goes to the heart of the problem.

In a typical Midwestern city, a company existed

that produced baked goods. They used all new equipment and the best raw materials to produce quality products. They had no competition, so they were not too concerned about overhead and labor costs. The company could charge whatever they wanted, but were cognizant enough to know the threshold of what people were willing to pay before going without. If people wanted to buy goods from a bakery they had no choice but to buy from the only company in town.

After a while, an entrepreneur who studied the situation decided that he could produce the same quality baked goods for a much lower price simply by buying used equipment, negotiating lower prices for raw materials, and by putting more efficient processes in place that required less labor. He soon opened a bakery and it wasn't long before his profits surpassed his competition. This was a benefit to the townspeople because now they had a choice as to where to buy their baked goods.

Well, the first company was not going to have any of this. Rather than taking a look at their own business practices, they decided to lobby a government agency in hopes of finding someone that would support their cause. They met with their suppliers and came up with a plan. Their representatives went to Washington and offered support and money to lobbyists and Political Action Committees that were affiliated with the agency responsible for regulating the baking industry. They complained that their competition did not use new equipment and that they paid a discount for raw materials. Therefore, they could not possibly produce products to the same high quality standards. They said that their competition used an outdated process that put the health of their workers and customers at risk. Subsequently, a regulation specifying standards for bakeries was passed along with all the red tape (paper work) that goes with it. Since the smaller bakery could no longer compete, it went out of business.

Of course the real losers were the townspeople who no longer had a choice as to where they could buy their baked goods. In the end, the company that caused all the havoc also lost because of the cost to comply with the regulation they so vigorously pursued and funded.

The above is a simple example, but it illustrates the point. When environmentalists, special interest groups, large corporations and anyone that promotes an agenda gets involved, the scenarios become much more complex.

The Hill recently noted that there were 3,378 final rules and regulations passed in 2015.[1] It also said that another 2,334 proposed rules were issued or are at various stages of consideration.

What is revealed next is staggering. *Ten Thousand Commandments* is an annual publication of current federal regulations.[2] The latest edition, published in 2015, states that

"Federal regulation and intervention cost American consumers and businesses an estimated $1.88 trillion in 2014 in lost economic productivity and higher prices." This amounted to an average of $14,976 per household or around 29 percent of an average family budget. Paid for with your hard earned money, the cost of regulation exceeds the amount an average family spends on health care, food and transportation. The costs amounted to more than the Internal Revenue Service was expected to collect, in both individual and corporate income taxes, by more than $160 billion. The current fiscal year may yield different numbers, but that does not change the enormity of the issue. There are currently more than a million rules and regulations listed in the journal. With over regulation there are always winners and losers. Most of the time the winners are the powerful while people who are just trying to make a living or run a small business have no choice but to pay the price.

Although regulations are often required to make sure laws are carried out properly, the current situation is ludicrous - worse than a run-a-way train. Every time a new rule or regulation is passed, there is a cost to U.S. citizens which results in fewer choices regarding how they conduct their lives and/or businesses.

Competition

"Competition may help us create better products and services, but in the end competition really seeks to destroy the opponent. To put him out of the power to compete against you." - Bangambiki Habyarimana, *The Great Pearl of Wisdom*

Competition is the basis of a capitalist society, where a country's trade and industry are controlled by private owners for profit rather than by the state. Consumers benefit as it enables them to choose from an abundance of excellent products at affordable prices. Companies also benefit as it encourages adoption of innovation, resulting in new ideas and products that will allow them to possibly gain a competitive advantage.

Private business prevailed in America up until the 18th century. During that time corporations did exist, but were chartered and controlled by the government, mostly for large infrastructure projects and to limit liability.[1] Sometime late in the 18th century corporations transitioned from being government affiliated entities to being public and private economic entities free of government direction.

The power of corporations rose substantially

when the Supreme Court in 1886, (relying on the Fourteenth Amendment) ruled that "A private corporation is a *natural person* under the U.S. Constitution, and consequently has the same rights and protection extended to persons by the Bill of Rights, including the right to free speech."[2] The consequences of this action are no more apparent than in today's lobbyist industry.[3] Hundreds of millions of dollars are spent by corporations annually as they try to influence politicians for their own gains, something that a *natural person* does not have the means to do. The ruling paved the way for corporations to use their wealth to dominate public thought, discourse, and allowed them to donate millions of dollars to political candidates.

Antitrust laws (beginning with the Sherman Antitrust Act of 1890) that regulate the conduct and organization of business corporations are used to promote fair competition for the benefit of consumers.[4] Corporations have always tried to exploit these laws to gain a competitive advantage in their respective marketplace. As a result, additional anti-trust laws have been passed over the years to ensure that competition continues to thrive.

One way that corporations try to get around antitrust laws is through consolidation; by means of mergers and acquisitions. Current federal law allows corporations to merge providing that it does not substantially lessen competition, or does not tend to create a monopoly. Mergers in the banking, airlines, health care, dairy, oil, drug and many other industries are increasing at alarming rates as companies try to corner their respective markets.[5] In addition, large corporate groups are forming to take control of these industries. Supposedly, as long as there are at least two large corporate groups in the same industry, competition still exists.

What does all this mean for the consumer and for small business? For the consumer, the answer is obvious. Less competition means less choice of products and eventually higher prices. For example, we are all experiencing the recent rise in prices for dairy, poultry, eggs and certain meats. Since many of these groups operate throughout the world, it could also mean shortages and inferior products if war or civil unrest breaks out where they operate.

For an entrepreneur that wants to start a small business the picture is bleak. Historically, small business creates about two-thirds of our nation's new jobs. According to a 2015 Washington Post article, "The rate of new business creation, which peaked about a decade ago, plunged more than 30 percent during the economic collapse (in 2007-2008) and has been slow to bounce back following the recession."[6] How much of this is due to corporate growth versus the "Great Recession" is debatable. What is known for sure is that large corporations typically bounce back much quicker than small businesses during a recession. Banks are more likely to loan to large corporation rather than to a small business because there is less risk. As corporations and corporate groups continue to grow and gain power, the choices become fewer for owners of small companies that are squeezed out of business. They can either try to find work at another company or with one of the growing number of government agencies.

Trade

"A fair bargain leaves both sides unhappy."
George R.R. Martin, *A Dance with Dragons*

The merits of free trade versus protectionism (tariffs) have been debated since before the country became a republic. Various tariff policies were tried through the first hundred years or so in an effort to protect "infant" or emerging industries. Economist Frank Taussig, found that tariffs did nothing to promote domestic industry stating, "Little, if anything, was gained by the protection which the United States maintained in the first part of the 19th century."[1] He concluded by saying, "The intrinsic soundness of the argument for protection to young industries therefore may not be touched by the conclusions drawn from the history of its trial in the United States, which shows only that the intentional protection of the tariffs of 1816, 1824, and 1828 had little effect."[2]

Nevertheless, more legislation was passed over the years. Most notably was the McKinley tariff in 1890 and the Payne-Aldrich tariff in 1909. The latter of which upset President William Howard Taft so much that he supported the 16th Amendment (as political payback) to the U.S. Constitution, thus creating a federal income tax.

Although protectionism continued, it began to weaken after World War II. Since then, globalization of the world economy has developed rapidly leading to what is known as free trade agreements (FTA's) and regional trade agreements (RTA's). The aim of a free-trade agreement is to reduce barriers, so that trade can grow as a result of specialization, division of labor, and most importantly via comparative advantage.[3]

Many conservatives view free trade agreements from a different viewpoint. That is, they see free trade agreements as the cause of lost jobs and high trade deficits. With the idea that tariffs supposedly don't work and that free trade supposedly doesn't work, it is not hard to see why there is so much debate. Nevertheless, the current trend is towards more free trade agreements.

From a pure deficit point of view, consider the following - According to the U.S. Census Bureau, the balance of payments on trade showed a deficit of over $530 billion for the year 2015.[4] So, are trade deficits bad? The Wall Street Journal stated in a June 8, 2015 article, "Running a trade deficit isn't necessarily bad. In the U.S. it can signal economic health: that American consumers and businesses are saving money buying cheaper foreign goods, and that the U.S. economy is attracting overseas investment, which drives productivity and demand for domestic and imported goods."[5] What the article fails to address is: - At what point do trade deficits start to become a detriment?

There is considerable rhetoric in the political arena about how deficits are bad because they create unemployment and run up the nation's debt. It is also said that we make bad trade agreements allowing counties to take advantage of us by devaluing their currencies. There may be some truth to this and it should be studied, but if the country slips back into a protectionism mode Americans will have no choice but to pay higher prices for goods and services.

More than three-quarters of all U.S. traded goods are manufactured products. Therefore, goods trade most directly affects manufacturing output and jobs. The Economic Policy Institute wrote, "The leading cause of growing U.S. trade deficits is currency manipulation, which distorts trade flows by artificially lowering the cost of U.S. imports and raising the cost of U.S. Exports. More than 20 countries, led by China, have spent about $1 trillion per year buying foreign assets to artificially suppress the value of their currencies (Bergsten and Gagnon 2012). Ending currency manipulation can create between 2.3 million and 5.8 million jobs for working Americans, and about 40 percent of those jobs (between 891,500 and 2.3 million) would be in manufacturing (Scott 2014)."[6]

Obviously, much work needs to be done regarding trade agreements. Until corrections are made in the favor of the American people, choices for goods manufacturing and other jobs are going to remain well below optimum.

The Food Supply

"Security for agriculture merits serious concern by not only the agricultural community but our nation as a whole. The risk to the U.S. food supply and overall economy is real." - Pat Roberts

Americans enjoy an abundance of food compared to many other parts of the World. They would like to believe that their food is safe and that the majority of it will continue to be supplied by our vast agricultural industry. The truth of the matter is that we have become a net importer of food products since the World Trade Organization conned us into signing the North American Free Trade Agreement (NAFTA) with Mexico and Canada in 1994.[1] That agreement promised new economic success for farmers and ranchers because of increased exports. It was believed that initial uneven import to export ratios and food prices would eventually level out in time. Instead, trade deficits ensued and food prices became volatile. In addition, a provision in the agreement required the elimination of various U.S. price support and supply management policies. The result has been devastating for small farmers as over 170,000 (21%) have disappeared. The story is the same with meat producers and the FTA (free trade agreement) with South Korea.[2] Meat exports have plummeted since the agreement was signed. In short, NAFTA and the FTA have been disasters. For whatever reason, international trade agreements never work out in our favor. Yet, consumers have no choice but to go along with them.

It is no secret that the cost of food and other products made from agricultural products is on the rise. In fact, food prices have risen 2%-3% a year since 1990.[3] Does accelerating food prices mean that our food supply is at risk because of shortages? Also, how safe is our food considering all that we are importing?

Known issues that affect America's food supply include - droughts in California, genetically modified crops that lead to fewer varieties and require more insecticides and fungicides, overabundance of corn grown for bio-fuel, food waste (estimated at 30% to 50%), energy dense foods (causing obesity and chronic disease), radiation from nuclear accidents, food-borne illnesses, overuse of growth hormones in beef, poultry, and dairy production, and ineffective oversight for imported foods.[4,5]

Let's take a look at an alarming issue that is emerging with regards to genetically modified crops. Large corporations are studying (and have produced) what are called terminator seeds. These are otherwise known as suicide seeds or "Genetic Use Restriction Technology." These are seeds that are genetically modified to naturally not reproduce. Although they are supposedly not being used in the U.S. yet, they are being used and field tested in other countries.[6] What this means is that farmers have no choice but to return to a particular company to buy seeds year after year rather than being able to harvest their own seeds or buy from a competitive market. Profits and elimination of competition are the driving forces behind these corporate actions. Fewer varieties, the possibility of cross contamination with non-genetically modified plants, and other concerns, raise serious questions regarding the use of these products.

The above issues definitely put our food supply at risk. Some would say that we have the choice to buy organic food, but that is a limited and more expensive choice. Besides, how do we know it is really organic food from non-GM sources? It is unsettling when we don't know how our food is produced, where it comes from or how it is going to affect our health.

Multinational corporations are taking over global food production in many categories. In February 2013, Britain's Independent ran a report that stated, "Putting too much power into the hands of too few companies' increases the risk of exploitation in food supply chains, where producers have no choice but to sell for low prices." It goes on to say, "Unless we do something now, millions of small farmers are condemned to poverty. If they are in crisis, and farmers see no future in farming, then many of our foods could be at risk."[7] This problem is only going to get worse as multinational corporations multiply and consolidate their power.

Our food supply has become such an important issue that the current administration has essentially nationalized it with Executive Order 13603.[8] Signed with little fanfare in March 2012, this order gives the Federal Government the power to take over the management and distribution of all food, water and other resources. The order puts emphasis on the confiscation of all "food resources," which are defined in the order as "all commodities and products, (simple, mixed, or compound), or complements to such commodities or products, that are capable of being ingested by either human beings or animals, irrespective of other uses to which such commodities or products may be put..." Some have interpreted this to mean that the government can take food from anyone who is storing it in their homes or in special locations for consumption in the event of an emergency.

How and where we buy our food is still our choice for now. What we buy is no longer our choice, and the idea that we may have no choice but to give up food that we have stored for an emergency is unconscionable.

Safety and Security

"Tradition becomes our security, and when the mind is secure it is in decay." - Jiddu Krishnamurti

It seems that with every passing administration, the safety and security of the American people are put at higher and higher risk. When illegal immigrants are allowed to flow through the borders unabated; when known terrorists are released knowing they will wreak havoc and put Americans around the world in danger again; when thousands of refugees from war torn countries are allowed to come into the country without verified vetting; when known terrorist cells are allowed to function in the homeland; when hard core criminals (some serving life sentences) have their sentences commuted; when protesters (turned to rioting) can destroy and loot property while the authorities are unable to do anything but stand by - our safety and security becomes more and more at risk. Does it sound like anything is wrong here? Is something amiss that we as a people have absolutely no control over? Are these incomprehensible occurrences precursors to widespread anarchy giving reason to implement martial law (probably under the guise of "a state of emergency") and the suspension of some, if not all, of Americans constitutionally protected rights - including the right to vote and hold national elections? In other words, by taking away choices that are the most basic to our freedom.

Consider this: On September 29, 2006, President George W. Bush signed the John Warner National Defense Authorization Act (NDAA) for fiscal year 2007 (H.R. 5122).[1] The law expanded the President's authority to declare martial law under revisions to the Insurrection Act, and actually allows the president to take charge of National Guard troops without state governor authorization. In 2011, President Obama used the 5112 NDAA to further strengthen the executive office's ability to declare martial law, and added provisions that would allow military troops to detain U.S. citizens without a trial.[2]

If the responsibility and the duty of the Federal Government is to protect our safety and security, then why is it creating and promoting conditions that could cause civil unrest? Why is it, in turn, passing and strengthening laws giving it supreme authority to take control of the country should civil unrest occur? Why is it not paying more attention to outside or inside radical influences that could cause mayhem and destruction of personal property or even death?

Declaring martial law would not set a new precedence as it has been used several times throughout our history. The most significant was probably during the Civil War. During that time, President Lincoln violated the Constitution (that he swore to uphold) many times.[3] He declared martial law in several states, suspended the writ of Habeas Corpus without the consent of Congress, shut down newspapers whose writers displayed any dissent to union policy or spoke out against him, raised troops without the consent of congress, and closed courts by force. He even imprisoned citizens, newspaper owners, and elected officials without cause and without a trial. Some would say that because of the times these things had to be done. Maybe so, but what is happening today is not the result of a civil war. What is happening today is unfathomable and reeks of something much more dangerous.

During the late 1960s virtually all police and National Guard troops were going through training exercises as a result of the race riots that sprung up across the country. Those exercises were mostly local and/or state sponsored. However, there were plans put in place by the Federal Government for the military to assist with further civil unrest should they be called upon. What is going on today goes much further.

Over the last few years there has been a number of homeland training exercises and military style drills that featured unmarked (other than with camouflage or white paint) military caravans of covered vehicles. Many of these exercises portray American citizens as the perceived threat.

In 2013, a Homeland Security-funded training exercise in Boston dubbed "Operation Urban Shield" revolved around a theoretical terrorist cell called "Free America Citizens."[4] Why is the DHS characterizing liberty-loving Americans as domestic extremists?

Also in 2013, the Ohio Army National Guard 52nd Civil Support Unit conducted a training drill where Second Amendment supporters with "anti-government" opinions were portrayed as domestic terrorists.

In 2015, Jade Helm, a large scale exercise that covered seven southwestern states over a six month period included some of America's most secretive units.[6] There is still much debate as to why these exercises were conducted.

There have been at least 20 such drills in the last two or three years. Most, if not all of these exercises include local police cooperation and/or involvement. More exercises are planned for 2016. What is going on? Why would American citizens be an imminent threat, possibly creating civil unrest? It makes one wonder if the police and military personnel are told or understand what the true purpose of these exercises is. What choices will they have to make regarding their neighbors and other U.S. citizens if civil unrest occurs?

The United States of America, that our founders so carefully created, has so eroded that it has become almost unrecognizable. It is being replaced by a system that has grown so powerful that most people don't even realize they could become enslaved by that very system.

Illegal Immigration

"A nation that cannot control its borders is not a nation." - Ronald Reagan

It is no secret that the southern U.S. border is open, allowing thousands of people to pour into the country illegally. Ironically, Congressmen on both sides of the aisle in Washington are not inclined or don't have the will to do anything about it. Although most support legal immigration, there are huge differences on how each side believes illegal immigrants and the security of our borders should be handled.

Liberals generally support amnesty for those that enter the U.S. illegally. They also believe that "undocumented immigrants" should have all the educational and health benefits that citizens receive including financial aid, welfare, social security, and Medicaid.

Conservatives are against amnesty for those who enter the U.S. illegally. They believe that those who break the law by entering the U.S. illegally do not have the same rights as those who enter legally and obey the law. They also believe that the Federal Government should do a better job enforcing current immigration laws.

Whether you call them "illegal immigrants" or you

call them "undocumented immigrants," the undisputed fact remains that when a person crosses the border without the proper authority, they are breaking U.S. immigration law. Just to be clear, there may be some immigrants that had green cards (or other legal authority) that either did not renew or replace an expired or lost card. This would be analogous to someone who let their driver's license expire and then proceeded to drive a car. They would be doing so illegally. Nevertheless, to put all illegal immigrants into the undocumented immigrant category is ludicrous.

It is estimated that there are between 11 and 30 million illegal immigrants in the country and that they account for 13.6% of all crime in the United States. No matter where you stand on this issue, the facts show that the direct and indirect financial costs are enormous. The following 2013 statistics were extracted from the website *fairus.org*.[1] Illegal immigration costs U.S. taxpayers about $113 billion a year at the federal, state and local level. Most of the costs (around $84 billion) are absorbed by state and local governments. That amounts to an average of $1,117 per household. The variance per household is higher or lower depending on the demographics of illegal alien populations. Education costs absorbed by state and local governments are estimated at $52 billion annually. Although illegal immigrants that work are required to pay income tax, most don't. Those that do get much of it refunded because they are in such a low income bracket.

According to the Bureau of Economic Analysis, illegal immigrants residing in the U.S. send $50 billion back to their home countries each year.[2] When you include legal immigrants, The World Bank estimates the amount to be $120 billion.[3] That is money that is not put back into the U.S. Economy.

According to National Review, $1.87 billion was spent in 2014 on incarcerating illegal criminal immigrants.[4] In 2009; the Department of Homeland Security estimated the percentage of illegal immigrants that are incarcerated to be between 11 and 15 percent of the country's prison population.[5] Almost all the financial burden was shouldered by the states. The State Criminal Alien Assistance Program (SCAAP), which is a federally funded program, does pay for some cost.[6] However, it does not really matter because it all comes out of taxpayer dollars.

The Government Accountability Office (GAO), using official Department of Justice data on criminal immigrants in the nation's correctional system, reported the following: - Between 2008 and 2014, 40% of all murder convictions in Florida were by criminal immigrants. In New York it was 34% and Arizona 17.8%. In addition, during those years, criminal immigrants accounted for 38% of all murder convictions in the five states of California, Texas, Arizona, Florida and New York.[7] That 38% represents 7,085 murders out of the total of 18,643.

It gets worse: Immigration and Customs

Enforcement (ICE) removed (deported) 235,413 criminal illegal immigrants nationwide in 2015, 49% percent of whom had previously been convicted of a criminal offense.[8] Although the numbers are down since 2012, they are still substantial. Do the reduced numbers mean that there are less illegal immigrants coming into the country or does it mean that ICE has less resources to do their job or does it mean they are told to stand down? In 2013 and 2014 ICE set free more than 66,000 illegal immigrant criminals who had over 166,000 convictions (30,000 for drunk or drug impaired driving, 414 kidnappings, over 11,000 rapes or other sexual assaults, and 395 homicides).[9] Since their release, many of those have already been convicted of new crimes including felonies.

It gets worse: The invasion of illegal immigrants has established and empowered many in the form of street gangs. Their growth is fueled by money obtained easily through drug smuggling and sales. A 2011 FBI report makes many connections between the Mexican drug cartels and various U.S.-based gangs.[10] An out of hand financial and social disruption cost to American citizens just continues to grow.

To make matters worse yet: Laws in sanctuary cities help shield illegal immigrants from deportation, despite astonishing statistics on violent crimes committed by illegal immigrants. These laws, in many cases, are in direct opposition to Federal immigration laws. Sadly, the U.S. Senate refuses to crack down on

America's nearly 300 sanctuary cities.

A 2014 Reuters article stated that a Reuters/Ipsos poll showed that 70% of Americans are deeply worried that illegal immigration is threatening the nation's culture and economy.[11] Concerns include job losses, the social landscape, how much insurance costs rise, and other related issues.

Since illegal immigrants typically take low skill, low paying jobs, it would be logical to surmise that some portion of those jobs are being taken away from legal immigrants. When that happens, few good choices remain for them. They are usually left with the choice to go back to their home country, get some kind of aid, or enter a life of crime.

Illegal immigration is totally out of control and our elected leaders know it. Securing the borders and fixing the illegal immigration problem should be demanded by the American people. Unfortunately, only about six percent of the population thinks it is a major problem (a sharp decline since 2014). They are either not aware of the enormity of the issue or they are more concerned about other issues.

The social landscape is rapidly changing and it puts all legal citizens at risk for the security of their families and homes. As a consequence, it reduces their choices as to where they live, shop, and travel.

Refugees

"Environmental degradation, overpopulation, refugees, narcotics, terrorism, world crime movements, and organized crime are worldwide problems that don't stop at a nation's borders." - Warren Christopher

The U.S. has a long and proud history of admitting refugees into the country. At the end of World War II, over 250,000 displaced Europeans were admitted and resettled in the U.S. The Displaced Persons Act of 1948 led to the admission of an additional 400,000.[1] Subsequent laws allowed persons to resettle that were fleeing from countries such as Hungary, Poland, Yugoslavia, Korea, China, and Cuba. Most of these refugees were assisted by private ethnic and religious organizations. The above actions resulted in little or no increase in crime rates and in fact contributed significantly to a booming economy after the war.

When Congress passed the Refugee Act of 1980, it standardized the resettlement services for all refugees admitted to the U.S. which led to today's U.S. Refugee Admissions Program[2]. Each year, the President of the United States consults with Congress and the appropriate agencies to determine what nationalities are eligible for refugee resettlement for the upcoming year. The

President also sets annual ceilings on the total number of refugees who may enter the country. Since 1975, the U.S. has resettled over 3 million refugees. The screening or vetting process for refugees is long and arduous and may take up to 2 years.[3]

Currently, there is a worldwide refugee crisis unfolding as a result of wars and chaos in the Mideast. The Islamic State (ISIS) is at the center, causing disruption and acts of terror around the world as they continue to build their caliphate. The impact on our communities and the American way of life (our choices) is unknown at this time. Nevertheless, there are reports that thousands of refugees are slated to be assimilated into hundreds of U.S. Cities. An Executive Memorandum dated November 21, 2014, called Creating Welcoming Communities and Fully Integrating Immigrants and Refugees led to the creation of the Task Force on New Americans.[4] The plan is to legalize 13 to 15 million illegal immigrants and/or refugees. In May 2015, Realside stated, "Under this memorandum, refugees planted in various communities are considered "seedlings" residing in, what will become, "receiving communities" which are entitled to benefits paid for by our tax dollars."[5]

What is disturbing is that most of these refugees do not have sufficient documentation to be vetted properly according to both the FBI and CIA directors.[6] They could easily be from terrorists or other groups that don't have the best interest of our nation in their hearts. Nevertheless, programs are being put into place by the current administration to fast track the process.

Interestingly, the entry of refugees can legally be stopped. Known as the McCarran-Walter Act, the Immigration and Nationality Act of 1952 allows for the "Suspension of entry or imposition of restrictions by the president.[7] It states, "Whenever the president finds that the entry of aliens or of any class of aliens into the United States would be detrimental to the interests of the United States, the president may, by proclamation, and for such period as he shall deem necessary, suspend the entry of all aliens or any class of aliens as immigrants or non-immigrants or impose on the entry of aliens any restrictions he may deem to be appropriate."

Besides the impact on the social landscape, the cost to American taxpayers is estimated to be over $55 billion, according to Senator Jeff Sessions, chairman of the Senate Judiciary Committee's Subcommittee on Immigration and the National Interest.[8] Additionally, refugees will be allowed to receive housing, welfare and food stamps.

It would seem reasonable that until the illegal immigration issue is solved, it would be wise not to be adding fuel to the fire and to the national debt by assimilating thousands of questionable refugees into the landscape.

Paternalism

"More than they wanted freedom, the Athenians wanted security. Yet they lost everything - security, comfort, and freedom. This was because they wanted not to give to society, but for society to give to them. The freedom they were seeking was freedom from responsibility. It is no wonder, then, that they ceased to be free. In the modern world, we should recall the Athenians' dire fate whenever we confront demands for increased state paternalism." - Margaret Thatcher

Paternalism - "A system under which an authority undertakes to supply needs or regulate conduct of those under its control in matters affecting them as individuals as well as in their relations to authority and to each other." - Merriam-Webster. Paternalism is the idea that an organization or the state believes it must nudge, limit, or take away a person's or group's liberty or self-autonomy for what is presumed to be that persons or groups own good. In other words, to make choices for you.

There are basically two types of paternalism. Soft paternalism says, "You know what's best for you and we will help you to do it." Soft paternalists say that it is feasible and valid for private and public institutions to affect behavior, providing freedom of choice is respected. They want to help (nudge) you to make choices that you would normally make for yourself (if only you were smart enough). Their aim is to affect your decisions without infringing greatly on your freedom of choice. For instance, in some states compulsive gamblers are given the choice to be put on a blacklist barring them from casinos for life. If they are caught in a casino, they are subject to arrest and loss of any winnings.

Hard paternalism says, "We know what's best for you and we will force you to do it." In other words, we will pass laws that take away any choice you may have had prior to the law. Good examples are seat belt and helmet laws. Mandatory contributions to Social Security and Medicare are other examples. In fact, hard paternalistic laws affect just about every aspect of our lives. Most of the time, the merits of these laws seem obvious despite the fact that your freedom to choose is taken away. There is a growing concern that as more laws are passed, the less freedom we will have to make choices. The question then is - At what point do we become a nanny state? That is, where the government overprotects and interferes unduly with personal choices. Some would say we are already there.

The Free Thought reports that, "Parents in the Magnolia [TX] Independent School district are furious after being threatened by police for picking up their kids from school — on foot."[1] An

MR Conservative article stated that in Louisiana, a church was recently ordered to stop giving out water because it did not have a permit to do so.[2] Another example described that in San Juan Capistrano (California) it is illegal to hold a home Bible study without a "conditional use" permit. These extreme examples confirm that the government and other interests believe that no matter what the problem is, there exists a legislative solution to fix it. They will keep trying to pass the perfect laws to make everyone better in every possible way.

There are thousands upon thousands of laws that limit, restrict, or take away our choices. There are so many in fact, that a person couldn't possibly know all the ones that exist in their own community let alone at the state or federal level. Advances in technology and other dynamics will surely spawn more. Mandating the use of electric and autonomous cars are two that come to mind. Good or bad, as long as these types of laws keep getting passed, we will lose more and more choices.

Crime

"When a man is denied the right to live the life he believes in, he has no choice but to become an outlaw." - Nelson Mandela

There is no question that crime is running rampant in America. The FBI reports that for the period 2014-2015, violent crime, murders and rape rates are up 1.75%, 6.2%, and 1.1%, respectively.[1] The tangible and intangible costs to society for these and all other crimes is a hard number to define, but estimates have put the number at over a $1 trillion dollars annually.

Crime can be found in virtually every community in America, although it is more prevalent where you find declining neighborhoods and poverty. Not all types of crimes thrive in poverty stricken areas, but there is certainly more overall social related crime in areas where economic conditions suffer. You also find high crime and misdemeanors of misconduct peculiar to officials, such as perjury of oath, abuse of authority, bribery, fraud, misuse of assets, failure to supervise, dereliction of duty, conduct unbecoming, and refusal to obey a lawful order in these as well as in the more affluent areas of the country.

Do people involved in crime consciously choose a

life of crime? Do children grow up thinking, - *Gee, I can't wait to start my life of crime.* Inherently not, but those that study this issue believe that a social environment where there are weak or broken bonds of family, school, and religion often leads to criminal behavior. Those who enter that lifestyle do not or cannot adhere to conventional social values and believe crime is the only way to improve their social condition. They believe that society has failed them at all levels. Consequently, many choose to join gangs as a replacement for family, to have protection, and as a way to make money. Gang members use their affiliation to make money through illegal activities, such as selling drugs and auto theft. Almost always, these are the only choices gang members have considering their situation.

Furthermore, Crime prevents businesses from thriving by generating instability and uncertainty. As a result, people often choose not to start a business in crime laden precincts.

Recently, we have seen incidents where businesses are broken into, looted and burned in conjunction with a protest that had nothing to do with them. The businesses just happened to be in the vicinity of the protest. For whatever reason, to make their point, protesters chose to take out their frustrations by causing violence and chaos. Whether protesters are encouraged by hate groups or for personal reasons, this is becoming their modus operandi.

Other types of crimes that are affecting many

Americans are computer related crimes. The rise of identity theft, cyber fraud, and ransom-ware are especially troubling. In fact, in 2013, incidents of identity theft alone were 60% higher than violent crime.[2] Nothing is sacred when it comes to identity theft and sometimes it can take months to resolve. Anything from tax refunds to credit cards to medical payments are all fair game. Total financial losses are estimated to be in the tens of billions of dollars.

Many companies collect and share personal information. Those that do are required to send out privacy notices.[3] Many times these go unnoticed. After all, who reads privacy notices? What is important to understand is that you can choose to opt out of having your information shared. You generally have 30 days to do so and after that you no longer have a choice. Once information is shared, it can end up anywhere, making it more vulnerable to identity theft.

Crime at some time or another affects all Americans. It often affects the choices that citizens can or cannot make in their lives. Therefore, supporting crime fighting and community revitalization efforts should be a priority for everyone.

Drugs

*"Whether you sniff it, smoke it, eat it, or
shove it up your ass the result is the same:
addiction."* - William S. Burroughs

A June 2015 survey, by The National Institute on
Drug Abuse, showed that an estimated 24.6
million Americans aged 12 or older or 9.4 percent
of the population had used an illicit drug in the
past month.[1] The cost to society which includes
lost productivity, health care and legal costs,
exceeds $190 billion.[2] Beyond the financial cost,
the cost to individuals, families and society
includes the spread of infectious disease, deaths
due to overdose, effects on unborn children,
crime, and homelessness.

Many reports confirm that the overwhelming
amount of illicit drugs enter the county through
the border with Mexico. This is despite the
rhetoric coming out of the current administration
that the southern border is secure. The Mexican
drug cartel organizations aren't only smuggling,
but they also traffic heroin, methamphetamine,
cocaine, and marijuana throughout the United
States. National and neighborhood gangs
continue to form relationships with what the
Federal Government coins as Transitional
Criminal Organizations (TCOs) to increase profits
through drug distribution and transportation. On

top of it all, there are drug cartels actually operating in the United States. Their organizations are growing so fast and are so wide spread that the Drug Enforcement Agency (DEA) cannot keep up. To put the problem in perspective, between 2010 and 2013 deaths from heroin overdose increased by 172%.[3]

There are many reasons people start on illicit drugs. It could be to soothe or avoid physical or psychological pain or escape from their lives, for reasons ranging from trauma to boredom. It may be ill advised, but most of the time it is a conscious choice.

Many believe that drug addiction is a disease. They say that addiction is a disease because of brain changes, evidenced by brain scans that cause the behavior known as addiction. Many things cause diseases, but the fact remains that addiction can be prevented by choosing not to use hard drugs or not to abuse prescription drugs. Once addiction occurs, there no longer is a choice as the drug takes over a person's life. The only choices left for them are to seek help or to figure out how to pay for their habit.

Many people are of the belief that selling hard drugs should not be considered a violent crime and that we should do away with mandatory sentences. In July 2015, the current administration released several dozen convicted felons, some of which were serving life sentences for pushing hard drugs. More are scheduled to for release this year. Bill OReilly, from Fox news, argues that dealing hard drugs is, in fact, a violent crime and should be met with harsh mandatory sentences.[4] Whether you call it a violent crime or a non-violent crime; it is just a matter of semantics. The damage to the country that results from hard drug use is indisputable. Therefore, sentences should remain harsh for those dealing, whether you call it a violent crime or not.

Along with illicit drug abuse, prescription drug abuse in America is also a growing dilemma. If you take a medicine in a way different from what the doctor prescribed, it is called prescription drug abuse. This includes taking medicine that is prescribed for someone else, taking a larger dose than prescribed, taking medicine by crushing tablets and then snorting or injecting them, and using medicine for other purposes, such as getting high.

A 2015 Talbot Recovery report stated that, "The United States makes up 5% of the world's population and consumes 75% of the world's prescription drugs."[5] It also reported that, "In the U.S. alone, more than 15 million people abuse prescription drugs." The most abused prescription drugs are painkillers, tranquilizers, depressants, and stimulants. Unlike illicit drug users that get most of their drugs off the street, 54.2% of prescription drug users get them free from a friend or relative. Many doctors contribute to the issue by prescribing the wrong or over prescribing a drug, especially when it comes to pain pills. This is because the education and expertise of many doctors are heavily influenced by pharmaceutical companies.[6] Trusting patients unknowingly have no choice but to take these drugs to ease their pain. To make matters worse, doctors are rarely screened or held accountable for prescribing the wrong drug or over prescribing.

Deaths caused by illicit as well as prescription drugs are growing at a substantial rate.[7] The associated costs are skyrocketing with no end in sight. The war on drugs is failing and the people of this country are paying a high price.[8]

The Grievance Industry

"Passionate hatred can give meaning and purpose to an empty life. Thus people haunted by the purposelessness of their lives try to find a new content not only by dedicating themselves to a holy cause but also by nursing a fanatical grievance. A mass movement offers them unlimited opportunities for both." - Eric Hoffer

Tolerance has all but disappeared in America. It has been replaced by a growing and dangerous industry based on grievance. Race related, abortion related, religion related, politically related, it does not matter. It seems that everyone has a grievance about something. You see it in schools, businesses, politics, and on the street. Debate and cooperation are not included in the lexicon of the grievance industry. Instead, we see silencing tactics, grievance filings, threats, protests, and shouting - some leading to violence and destruction of personal property. Most Americans are appalled at what they see, yet the grievance industry continues to grow.

Nowhere is it more apparent than on college campuses and in the workplace.[1] Make an innocent remark, look at someone slightly the wrong way, or be in the wrong place at the wrong time and you could have a grievance filed against you. No one is immune. Not business supervision, not workers, not college administrators, not professors, and not students. It does not matter whether there was malicious intent or not - the result could be unpaid time off, dismissal or expulsion. To protect themselves, colleges and businesses are spending millions of dollars on lawyers to settle grievances and avoid lawsuits. If you are on a college campus or at your workplace, you have no choice but to be very careful about what you say and what you do.

Hate groups spawned by both far right and far left activists grew substantially over the last decade. Many have existed for some time, while others arise out of opposition and anger related to newly formed fringe movements and certain ideologies.[2] A recent Washington Post article indicated that a number of factors for inciting that anger include shifting demographics, immigration, legalized same-sex marriage, the rise of the Black Lives Matter movement, and atrocities carried out by Islamic terrorists.[3] To be clear on this issue, the grievance industry does not discriminate. It thrives on all groups (ideologically left or right), whether it is a small fringe movement or a highly radicalized group.

Funding and support for hate groups can and does come from anywhere. Billionaire businessmen, corporations, politically affiliated groups, and many other organizations all provide funds for the purveyors of hate. They recruit by targeting disenchanted youths who are abused, angry, unemployed, dropouts or runaways, and even children who may be looking for someone to blame for their problems. Often, they protest without even knowing what they are protesting. This is especially true with political protests. It is sad that people feel they have no choice but to join hate groups as a way to display their frustrations and vent their anger.

So, where does all this hate, divisiveness, and vicious atmosphere come from? Some say it is from an administration that seems to want to divide the country on every issue. Others say it is created by the rhetoric of political candidates and parties. Some say it is caused by the news media. There probably is a bit of truth to all the above. One thing for sure, the grievance industry is not suffering from any of it. The only ones that are suffering are the American people.

Those that choose to join hate groups because they have lost their tolerance and faith in the American dream, suffer. Those that choose to believe the propaganda perpetrated by hate groups, suffer. Those that choose to get caught up in the often occurring violence associated with hate groups, suffer. Most of all, the country suffers because the rest of the world sees us not as a cohesive people that share similar values and principles, but as a country that is divided, full of hate, and has begun to question our very own ability to lead and govern.

Big Government

"If your answer to every failure of government is more government, you're like an alcoholic trying to drink yourself sober." - Will Spencer

The first question that needs to be asked is, "Are we a government or are we a state?" According to FEE, The Foundation for Economic Education, "A government is the consensual organization by which we adjudicate disputes, defend our rights, and provide for certain common needs." Whereas, "A state, on the other hand, is a coercive organization asserting or enjoying a monopoly over the use of physical force in some geographic area and exercising power over its subjects."[1] With that understanding, it begs a second question, "When does a government get so big and powerful that it becomes a state? Thomas Jefferson once wrote, "The natural progress of things is for liberty to yield and government to gain ground." Since we elect politicians who are just as self-interested as the rest of us, it should be no surprise that they are probably not going to act in the interest of the public. This could explain voting patterns, lobbying efforts, deficit spending, corruption, the expansion of government, and the opposition of lobbyists and members of Congress to term limits.

The bigger a government gets the more corrupt and inefficient it gets. It seems that when an issue arises in the country and the government does not know how to handle, it must form another agency. According to the Federal Register there are around 440 federal agencies in the Federal Government.[2] The programs these agencies administer often overlap, leading to fragmented, duplicate, and inefficient efforts costing billions of taxpayer dollars.

In September 2015, CNS News reported that there were 21,995,000 people employed by the federal, state and local governments in the United States.[3] Compare this to just 12,329,000 people employed in the manufacturing sector. The Federal Government overtook manufacturing as a U.S. employer in 1989 and has continued to grow while manufacturing jobs continue to decline.

The bigger the government grows the less citizens trust it. They simply don't trust that a new law was made fairly or independently or in some cases even democratically. They doubt that the result was based on facts and question the conviction of politicians. Voters distrust government so much that they are not willing to accept the results of virtually any decision made by the political process. Why? Maybe it is because the government is becoming more obtrusive in our lives. It exercises power over us by limiting or even eliminating choices that used to be taken for granted.

Interestingly, there is a dichotomy that exists among our culture. There are those that are deeply concerned over a growing and overbearing government and then there are those that want the government to take more control. The latter believes that government should redistribute wealth and provide more for its citizens. Free health care and free college are two examples that come to mind.

Throughout history, no free nation has ever thrived when it went from a capitalist democracy to a socialist state. Yet, most working examples of socialism today are supported by capitalism and visa versa. The imbalance between the two determines whether people are going to have the ability to make more choices or fewer choices. Those that favor socialism should consider these words from Winston Churchill, "Socialism is a philosophy of failure, the creed of ignorance, and the gospel of envy, its inherent virtue is the equal sharing of misery"

Debt

"After a decade of profligacy, the American people are tired of politicians who talk the talk but don't walk the walk when it comes to fiscal responsibility. It's easy to get up in front of the cameras and rant against exploding deficits. What's hard is actually getting deficits under control. But that's what we must do. Like families across the country, we have to take responsibility for every dollar we spend." - Barack Obama

Isn't it ironic that the above quote came from a man whose administration saw the gross national debt double in less than eight years? That is more than the total debt increase of all previous presidents. It now stands at over $19 trillion, more than $58,000 for each person that lives in the U.S. Granted, this president came into office just after the beginning of the "Great Recession."[1] Drastic steps were required, that cost U.S. taxpayers trillions of dollars, to bail out those responsible and help straighten out the economy. Nevertheless, after almost eight years the fiscal irresponsibility of this nation continues.

The last time that the U.S. ran a surplus was in the years from 1998-January 2001.[2] The total was a little over $558 billion. In 1999 the national debt stood at about $5.7 trillion.[3] At the time it was estimated, that with responsible fiscal policy reforms, the surplus would continue to grow and the debt could be paid off by 2015.[4] By the end of 2015 the national debt stood at over $18 trillion.[5] So much for fiscal responsibility. Whenever there is a rare opportunity to pay down the national debt, it is squandered on more irresponsible spending. It is not a matter of whether a fiscal crisis will come or not, as it surely will if things don't change. Just take at what is happening in Europe.[6]

The gross national debt is the debt held by the public combined with securities the Treasury issues to U.S. government trust funds.[7] Public debt is what the government borrows from the private sector (including banks and investors) and foreign governments. Currently, public debt makes up about 75% of the total debt. The other 25% of the debt is created by bookkeeping wizardry. When there is a surplus in one part of the government, it issues treasuries to replace the surplus and uses the funds to pay for other operations. In other words, it writes and IOU. The theory is that the money will be paid back (by the government) when the bonds come due.

For instance, all the assets in the Social Security trust funds are held in "special issue" securities.[8] Now, here is the kicker. These securities are not sold to, traded, or redeemed by the public. The securities held in Social Security trust funds have to be paid back (including interest) with other government receipts, which can only come in the form of taxes, money printing or borrowing. In other words, there is no cash in the trust funds and the money to redeem the special issues securities has to be paid by a government that is broke. The story of how this happened is long and complex. More information can be found here.[9]

It gets worse: Currently the annual budget deficit is running at over $500 billion.[10] That is how much money is being spent over what revenue is expected to be received through income generating activities in a given year. This is money that has to be borrowed and added to the total gross national debt. Furthermore, it has been reported that the Federal Government wastes as much as $1 trillion a year.[11] If half the waste could be eliminated, so would the annual budget deficit.

It gets worse: Unfunded liabilities now stand at over $100 trillion, or over $852,000 per taxpayer.[12] Defined by Investors World, unfunded liabilities are: "The amount, at any given time, by which future payment obligations exceed the present value of funds available to pay them."[13] The amount includes, among others, the U.S. federal budget deficit, Social Security liability, and Medicare Liability.

It gets worse: State and local debts are currently over $3 trillion.[14]

When we add personal debt to the picture, it gets worse yet. Total personal debt, which includes mortgages, student loans, and credit cards now stands at over \$18 trillion.[15] That is almost equal to the size of the total gross national debt.

No one is left unscathed by the burden of a seemingly insurmountable debt. Not the federal, state, or local governments, not corporations, not small business, and not citizens. Of course, there is always the risk of default at some point in time. But, before that happens, it is possible that we would see higher taxes, higher costs for food and commodities, higher interest on loans, possible loss of government benefits, more job losses, and recession (or worse). As a result, the choices that we are able to make will become more limited and totally out of our control.

The Federal Reserve

"Give me control of a nation's money and I care not who makes its laws." - Mayer Amschel Bauer Rothschild

The Federal Reserve Act was signed into law on December 23, 1913 by President Woodrow Wilson.[1] Its purpose was to establish an independent central banking system for the nation. The Federal Reserve's function is to hold the cash reserves of depository institutions, make loans, and give credit to them. In addition, it moves currency and coin into and out of circulation, collects and processes checks, and provides checking accounts for the treasury. It also supervises and examines member banks for safety and soundness. Finally, it sets monetary policy for the country and provides certain financial services to the U.S. government, U.S. financial institutions, and foreign official institutions. There are currently 12 Federal Reserve districts spread across the country that provide those services.[2]

Contrary to what many people believe, the Federal Reserve is not a government agency. It is an independent entity within government that is set up like a private corporation. Also, it does not print currency or mint coin. That is done by the U.S. Treasury Department - Bureau of Engraving and Printing, and the U.S. Mint. The Federal Reserve buys physical currency at cost (for labor and materials) and distributes it for the Treasury Department to depository institutions (member banks). Interestingly, the currency printed by the U.S. Treasury is called a Federal Reserve Note, not a United States Note.

So, what is wrong with the above picture? First, Article 1 of the Constitution states that: "Congress shall have the Power to Coin Money and Regulate the Value Thereof." In other words, the Federal Congress should have the power to create and control money and that power should not be put in the hands of independent bankers, but that is exactly what happened with the passage of the Federal Reserve Act. Second, the Federal Reserve pays a subsidy in the form of a 6 percent dividend on stock that over 2,900 member banks purchase (at a fixed cost) to participate in the Federal Reserve system.[3] Member banks have been collecting dividends for over 100 years. In 2012 the Federal Reserve paid out over $1.64 billion in dividends. This all goes on while American citizens have no choice but to earn less than 1% on their own savings accounts.

Why does all this matter? As we saw earlier, the Federal Government borrows money from many sources. As you may have guessed, it also borrows from the Federal Reserve. Well, not exactly. The government does this by auctioning U.S. Treasuries that are purchased by member banks of the Federal Reserve. In turn, the Federal Reserve issues credit and records the value of the Treasuries on its balance sheet. Member banks are able to loan out 90% of the value of the Treasuries. When the loans are paid back, they can loan out 90% again. They can do this over and over up to 10 times. Technically, the U.S. government must pay the Federal Reserve back one day (when the Treasuries are redeemed), supposedly with taxpayer dollars. Currently, the Federal Reserve owns $2.5 trillion worth of Treasuries.[4] This is considered debt owed to the public by the government even though the securities are actually owned by an independent entity within government.

Why doesn't the Government just use the money it prints? The answer is because there is much more to the money supply than just physical currency.[5]

People would like to believe that how they choose to save or spend their money is in their control. The truth is that the Federal Reserve totally controls those choices. By adjusting interest rates up or down, it influences mortgage rates, auto loan rates, credit card rates, and so on. It also indirectly affects a person's ability to maintain employment and buy goods and services.

The Federal Reserve has tremendous power, yet it has never been audited, despite a Senate bill that would start the process.[6] It failed by a vote of 53-44. It would behoove all Americans to keep an eye on what is happening with the Federal Reserve.

The Economy

"Until you realize how easily it is for your mind to be manipulated, you remain the puppet of someone else's game." - Evita Ochel

Although America has had a long and rich economic history, it has not gone without its tremulous times. Starting out as a marginally successful colonial economy, it grew into a small independent farming economy as the country spread westward. Using the Constitution for its basis, the government began to regulate commerce with foreign nations and the states fairly early. It established uniform bankruptcy laws and created and regulated the value of money. Tariffs on foreign trade were instituted with the creation of the first secretary of the treasury (Alexander Hamilton) and the first national bank was chartered in 1791. As time went on, the economy evolved to a highly complex industrial economy with increased government involvement.

The Industrial Revolution, which began around 1860, lead to 16 percent of the U.S. population living in urban areas. After the Civil War, industry in the north expanded rapidly and came to dominate many aspects of the nation's economy, including social and political affairs.

Late in the 19th century there was an explosion of new discoveries and inventions. Oil was discovered and by the dawn of the 20th century, cars and airplanes became common sights. It wasn't long before a third of the nation's income came from manufacturing. The emergence of private corporations triggered the rise of organized labor to counter the power and influence of business. Subsequently, anti-trust laws were passed to preserve competition and many of today's U.S. regulatory agencies were created.

The Federal Reserve Bank was created in 1913 and within 16 years, it all came crashing down. It has been written that the monetary policies of the Federal Reserve caused the Great Depression that lasted from 1929 to about 1939.[1] When President Franklin D. Roosevelt launched the new deal to help alleviate the emergency, government involvement in the economy increased significantly. The legislation that followed was intended to extend federal authority in banking, agriculture, and public welfare. One short-lived initiative, The National Industrial Recovery Act, sought to encourage business and labor to resolve conflicts thereby increasing productivity and efficiency. Although it failed, the government continued to grow as it intervened extensively in the economy.

After the country was drawn into World War II, the government intervened again when most industries were converted to making war material. A pent up demand for consumer goods pursued after the end of the war and by 1960 the gross domestic product more than doubled. The government continued to accelerate economic growth by increasing spending and cutting taxes. Upon the death of President John F. Kennedy, federal spending increased substantially as the government instituted new social programs such as Medicare, Food Stamps and numerous education initiatives. As taxes were cut further and more social programs were launched, the national debt grew, resulting in recessions about every 10 years (1980, 1990, and 2000).

Then, late in 2007 an $8 trillion bubble burst. It was not caused by war, food or product shortages or bad international trade deals. Unprecedented increases in household debt, greed, and risky financial practices by mortgage and investment companies was the cause.[2] With rating companies distorting the value of bonds and the absence of government oversight, the economy almost totally collapsed. Many choices for Americans either ceased to exist or became severely limited during the peak years (2007 - 2009) of what is now referred to as "The Great Recession." During that time, labor markets lost 8.4 million jobs (6.1%), consumer spending and business investment dried up, poverty increased, and the drop in the stock market lead to a drop in family wealth.[3] Today the economy continues to stagnate as the gross domestic product struggles along at .5% for the first quarter of 2016.[4] A healthy rate is considered to be between 2% - 3%.[5]

Despite nursing a recovery that is still lagging, the United States accounts for nearly 18% of the world's gross domestic product and it continues to slowly grow.[6]   This is a testament to the country's resilience, fundamental strengths, and ability to overcome adversity despite all its problems.   Nevertheless, the warning signs of economic decline, discussed earlier, are more prevalent than ever.

Crucial choices lay ahead for Americans. Choices that involve electing, and holding accountable, leaders that understand what affect government actions and initiatives have on the economy. That is, leaders who understand that government is a business and should be treated like a business.   Americans must seek leaders that understand the root causes of the problems facing the country, so that they can make well informed decisions in the years ahead. Those choices are critical.   They must be the right choices because there is no more room for mistakes or partisan politics. Choosing the right leaders will not be an easy task, as we shall see later.   But, Americans must make the right choices because the stakes have never been higher.

Taxes

"We contend that for a nation to try to tax itself into prosperity is like a man standing in a bucket and trying to lift himself up by the handle." - Winston C. Churchill

Federal and state income taxes, sales taxes, fuel taxes, capital gains taxes, utility taxes, vehicle registration tax, luxury taxes, social security taxes, Medicare taxes, health care taxes, real estate taxes, school taxes, various permit taxes, local unemployment taxes, state revenue stamps, and on, and on, and on. If this is not enough to make your head spin, consider that there have been 4,428 changes to the federal tax code alone over the decade ending in 2013.[1] Trying to tally up all the various taxes that Americans pay to all levels of government is a hopeless task. In fact, there are so many types of taxes, it would be near impossible to determine and list them all. Instead, let's see who pays what, how liberals and conservatives think, and how your quality of life and the choices you make are affected.

A 2016 Pew Research Center report stated that in 2014 people with adjusted gross incomes above $250,000 paid just over half (51.6%) of all federal individual income taxes.[2] By contrast, people with incomes of less than $50,000 paid just 5.7% of total taxes. When all other sources of federal revenue (such as payroll taxes that fund Social Security and Medicare, excise taxes such as those on gasoline and cigarettes, estate taxes, customs duties, and payments from the Federal Reserve) are factored in, the top 0.1% of families pay the equivalent of 39.2% and the bottom 20% have negative tax rates. That is, they get more money back from the government in the form of refundable tax credits than they pay in taxes. Looking at it a different way, the top 20% of earners pay a whopping 86% of taxes.[3] When all federal, state and local taxes are considered (many of which are hidden), it has been estimated that Americans pay an average of over 50% of their earned income in taxes.[4] Nevertheless, the debate rages on concerning regarding whether the rich are paying their fair share.

Liberals say no and believe that higher taxes (primarily for the wealthy) are necessary to address inequity/injustice in society. That is, the government should help the poor and needy using tax dollars from the rich. Liberals support a large government to provide for the needs of the people and create equality. They believe that more taxes enable the government to create jobs and provide welfare programs for those in need.

On the other hand, conservatives believe lower taxes and a smaller government with limited power will improve the standard of living for all citizens. Conservatives believe that lower taxes create more incentive for people to work, save, invest, and engage in entrepreneurial endeavors. In other words, money is best spent by those who earn it, not the government. They say that government programs encourage people to become dependent and lazy, rather than encouraging work and independence.

Whatever your belief, the tax burden on American citizens continues to grow with no end in sight. Nowhere is this more apparent than with the Supreme Court ruling regarding the Affordable Care Act. On June 28, 2012, the Supreme Court declared that the Affordable Care Act was a tax and not a mandate, and was therefore declared constitutional.[5] When rising co-pays and deductibles are factored in, the costs are insurmountable. The result is that many people are not able to take advantage of the insurance.

The total tax burden on the American people is stifling. Unfortunately, we don't get an up or down vote on taxes other than for some state taxes and local millage's. The result is less money for discretionary spending. When discretionary spending decreases, so does our choices regarding how we spend and save. Thus, our lifestyle suffers a little more each time we have to pay new or higher taxes.

The United States has the highest statutory (before deductions) corporate tax rate in the world (35 percent at the federal level and 39.2% when state taxes are added on).[6] The World Bank and the International Finance Commission puts the United States' effective tax rate (after deductions) for 2014 at 27.9 percent, only second behind New Zealand.[7] This is causing many corporations to reincorporate and move some, if not all, of their operations out of the United States into nations with lower taxes. The official term for this practice is "tax inversion" or as some like to call it, tax evasion.

Corporations accomplish this by acquiring a foreign company of at least 25 percent of their own size. Corporations say they have no choice because the U.S. is one of the few countries that require that its companies pay taxes on all their worldwide income, making it harder to compete on a global basis. Considering that some of these companies make profits in the billions of dollars, some would say it looks more like greed than not being able to compete. This practice continues despite a 2004 law that promised to cut down on the inversions.[8]

Tax inversions have resulted in a significant decrease in federal tax revenue. A Bloomberg Quicktake article stated that in 1950, corporate taxes accounted for about 30% of all federal revenue.[9] In 2012, corporate taxes accounted for less than 7% of all federal revenue. It is currently estimated that over $2 trillion has been lost to date, and that number will increase to $19 trillion by the year 2024.[10]

Recently there has been talk of putting stiff tariffs on products imported from these companies. That would leave Americans with no choice but to pay higher prices for their products. It seems that a better solution would be to create an environment that would encourage companies to stay in the United States. If this trend is not reversed, could it mean that American citizens are going to have no choice but to pay higher taxes as corporate tax revenues continue to fall?

Health Care

"The health care bill is nothing about health care - it's about controlling the people." -
David Lincoln

Early in the 1800s, hospitals were a place to go to die rather than a place to get treatment for disease. When physicians learned enough about disease to be reliably helpful in treating sick people they banded together to create the American Medical Association (AMA) in 1847, becoming a powerful influence over health care legislation.[1] During the Civil War, doctors began charging more than most individuals could easily pay and the first rudimentary health insurance company was formed. This changed the way health care was delivered and paid from that point forward.

Early in the 1900s there was debate regarding whether health care should be mandatory. The AMA voiced strong opposition because the thought was that it would increase bureaucracy and limit the freedom of doctors. The Great Depression brought more debate regarding government based benefits. Near the end of the depression the Social Security Act was passed (creating a new, no choice, payroll tax), but it did not include health insurance.[2] Nevertheless, health insurance started appearing in more

109

states.

When wage controls were placed on employers during World War II, companies began to offer health insurance coverage to compensate employees. Thus, we had the beginning of the employer-based system in vast use today. Subsequently, President Harry Truman made a case for nationalizing health care, but the AMA voiced their opposition once again.[3] They deemed it "socialized medicine," and it did not gain support. Medicine continued to advance and the first successful kidney transplant was performed on December 23, 1954.[4] Disability benefits were included in Social Security that same year. Along with these advances came the doubling of health care costs.

Americans had no choice but to pay another payroll tax when President Lyndon Johnson signed Medicare into law in 1965. With it came a significant increase in companies offering private health insurance and more doctors began to specialize as a way to increase their earnings. As a result, the cost of health care continued to rise at an alarming rate. In an attempt to quell rising costs, the government intervened again in 1973 when President Richard Nixon signed the Health Maintenance Organization Act (HMO) into law. This law funded and promoted managed care by non-profit companies that could (if qualified) offer health insurance to an employee group. By the 1990s, Americans were left with few choices as employers moved most of their employees into managed care health insurance plans.

During the following years, despite more government initiatives, the cost of health insurance continued to rise, leaving millions of people to do without. From 2009 to 2015, World Bank statistics show that the U.S. had the highest health care costs relative to the size of its economy (GDP) in the world.[5] To make matters worse, it is estimated that 20–30% of health spending is wasted with no benefit to patients. Reasons include over treatment, failure to coordinate care, administrative complexity, and fraud.[6]

In what now seems like a last ditch effort to provide health care to millions of uninsured, control costs, and improve overall care, The Patient Protection and Affordable Care Act (PPACA) was passed in 2010. So far the PPACA has been a dismal failure in just about every sense of the word. The administration promised that if people liked their current health care plan and doctor they would be able to keep them. Pundits like to play with the numbers, but it is estimated that initially between 2.6 and 4.6 million people lost their health insurance.[7] They had no other choice. This number is estimated to rise substantially as the program continues to roll out.[8]

The administration promised that affordable insurance would be available to an estimated 50 million uninsured people. As of May 2016 there are still around 29 million people (about 9% of the population) without health care insurance.[9]

Truth is, those people can't afford to buy coverage, or can only afford to buy coverage with high out-of-pocket costs. Therefore, their only choice is not to buy it and pay a penalty. Those that are covered under PPACA are now seeing their premiums and deductibles increasing.[10] Many insurance companies are either forced to raise premiums or are opting out of the PPACA because they are simply not able to make a profit. So much for affordable. Although, there has been some improvement in the way health care is administered and delivered under the PPACA, the high costs outweigh them.

Government health care taxes and mandates have destroyed free-market insurance. Economic good sense does not exist in a mandate-controlled, third-party-payer system. As a result, people are left with fewer choices as health care costs rise. There are those that are promoting free health care, but they will have to explain how they plan to avoid a crushing tax and further debt burden on the American people.

Presidential Elections

"When one with honeyed words but evil mindpersuades the mob, great woes befall the state." - Euripides, Orestes

First things first - Political parties are private clubs whose members are elected to government positions[1]. They are not part of the government. Therefore, the so called primary election process has nothing to do with the government. Political parties are registered by each state. A Party that has an independent state organization in a majority of the states is listed as a major party. There are currently five such parties. Also, there are over 30 minority parties. What is important to understand is that the major parties registered in each state decide how they will choose a nominee. This can be done by having a primary vote, holding a caucus or in some cases by having county and state conventions where voters may or may not be involved.[2] In addition, the national committcc of each party sets the rules for the national convention.

Most would probably agree that the process to elect a new president is too demanding, too long, and too expensive. The top two candidates from the 2012 campaign spent a total of $2.6 billion on their campaigns.[3] The process takes around 18 months from the time a person announces their

113

candidacy. By the time the general election rolls around Americans are usually fed up and left to vote for one of two bad choices. Bad because in some cases the American people are left out of the process of choosing a nominee.[4] Bad because of campaign promises that can't or won't be kept. Bad because most candidates are bought and paid for by special interest groups that ultimately influence national policy. In fact, a 2014 study titled: Testing Theories of American Politics: Elites, Interest Groups, and Average Citizens - revealed that Americans have virtually no impact whatsoever on the making of national policy.[5]

The analysts found that policy outcomes are shaped by rich individuals and business-controlled interest groups, not by the views of common citizens. Rich individuals and business interests have the capability to hire lobbyists that fill the campaign coffers of political candidates. In addition, Political Action Committees (PACs) and Super PACs raise and spend large sums of money to elect or defeat candidates.

PACs have been around since 1944. Most represent business, labor or ideological interests. They have a limit of $5,000 that they can give to a candidate per election (primary, general or special). Additionally, they can give up to $15,000 annually to any national party committee, and $5,000 annually to any other PAC. PACs may receive up to $5,000 from any one source per calendar year.[6]

A July 2010 federal court decision in a case

known as *SpeechNow.org v. Federal Election Commission* led to the creation of Super PACs.[7] The function of Super PACs and how they raise money is basically the same as regular PACs. The difference is that they can raise unlimited amounts of money, but are prohibited from donating money directly to political candidates or coordinating spending with that of candidates.[8] Although sources of money for all PACs must come from U.S. interests, foreign money finds its way into PACs coffers through foreign subsidies located in the United States.

Lobbyists cannot give more than $5,000 to any Political Action committee per calendar year. However, they can give over $100,000 to national party committees. They can create charitable trusts that pay for their lobbying and campaign efforts (without disclosing where the money comes from – also known as dark money).[9] Also, they can work on campaigns and serve as the treasurer of a PAC. There were 11,504 lobbyists as of 2015 with total spending of $3.21 billion.[10] The committees that are led by lobbyist have spent in excess of $525 billion to influence the political process since 1998.[11,12]

PACs spend hundreds of millions of dollars on ads and use all available media to smear the opposing candidate or support their own. The spin doctors are experts at distorting the truth.[13] The result is that Americans do not get the truth or the chance to make an informed voting decision. It is just not possible, that choice has been taken away.

Because people are disenfranchised, they do not believe they have the ability to participate in the political process, therefore millions choose not to vote. The voter turnout rate in the U.S. is near the bottom of industrialized democracies. More than 90 million that were eligible to vote in the 2012 presidential general election did not vote.[14]

Grassroots movements that try to influence politicians are common in America, but they do not have near the influence of the civil rights and woman's movements of the 1960s and 1970s that changed the nation. Americans always do better getting the message across to Washington when they unite under a common cause. Today, grassroots movements are relatively small and tend to fizzle out over time due to lack of interest and support. It should come as no surprise that this is because the country has become divided and polarized.

This situation did not come about unintentionally. Those who study history know that the best way to control and quell political outrage is to first divide, polarize and then spin people into small ineffective groups. Small, meaning not in the interest of the masses. This is a very effective strategy as it keeps the people pitted against each other instead of against their oppressors. It is the oldest political scheme known to human civilization.

Have we reached a point of no return? There still may be time, but not more than one or two election cycles before our votes become totally ineffective. If this situation is to be corrected the American people must unite as one and demand that election and policy making processes be changed to benefit all Americans. The American people must unite to reclaim their democracy and their choices. They must unite to challenge the politicians who don't give a damn about anything but themselves. Will a new leader emerge that is willing to take on this challenge? Only time will tell.

The Establishment

"The history written, taught, and sworn to as 'the unvarnished truth' by the establishment—any establishment, left or right, conservative or liberal, capitalist or socialist or fascist—is generally revisionist, narrow in perspective, monolithic, and agenda-driven. In the worst case, it consists of one part denial and one part propaganda—in other words, a self-serving pack of lies." Thomas W. Knowles

Ah yes, the establishment; the primary source of power in a society. The implicit organization to which all politically minded people long to join, but few will confess to being a member. A never static eternal body that collects and discards members to serve its own continuing existence. The malleable and adaptive behemoth that would like us to believe that there are really two establishments. That is the Republican Establishment and the Democratic Establishment. After all, Americans are becoming more polarized, disliking the other party more and more, as they see the opposite party as a threat. Compromise is not an option as Americans on one side despise and distrust those on the other. As far as Americans are concerned, there is no more middle road. Nevertheless, political candidates on both sides stay politically correct by saying they will fight against the "Establishment."

So, just who or what is the establishment? The McClatchy-DC website interviewed several people asking the above question.[1] One of the respondents, was quoted as saying, "The establishment is anybody with big money who can get to the congressmen and lobbyists." Others believe it is a combination of both the Democratic and Republican members of Congress, along with the Wall Street bankers and the mainstream media. Since what Congress, (including the lobbyists that influence it), has the most effect on what choices we have (or don't have) in our lives, we'll use that as our definition.

In the past, liberals and conservatives in the establishment stood just to the left or the right of center along the political spectrum. Although they did not always agree on how to solve every issue, there was open debate and cooperation that lead to functional legislation. Today, most members of the establishment are polarized along ideological lines and the gap is getting wider. As the establishment becomes more polarized, so do the American people.

There is evidence that polarization has been progressing since Lyndon Johnson signed the Civil Rights and Voting Rights Acts in the mid-1960s, albeit not at the pace of the last decade. The result has been congressional gridlock which makes it difficult (at best) to pass laws and budgets that satisfy the needs of the people.[2]

Instead, we see a steady stream of committee meetings, inquiries, and hearings that take months and months to complete. We see Senate majority leaders that stifle debate and delay or keep legislation from coming to a vote.[3] We see Americans following suit who are intolerant of each other's viewpoint to the point that they would rather silence and demonize the other side than have a healthy debate on their differences.

There are many reasons for the decline of the establishment. One that cannot be ignored is the lack of leadership and disconnect of the current administration. Admittedly, the administration must perform many important functions, but that does not preclude the fact that one of the most important is to create a positive and cooperative atmosphere among all branches of government (something the current administration has clearly and sorely failed to do).

Many believe that no matter what it looks like from the outside, all members of the establishment belong to the same club. As polarized as it has become, one would think Congress would take action on issues that are common to both sides, but it continually fails to do so. Why is that? Some say that it is due to the lack of trust between the administration and the establishment.[4] In other words, they know when legislation crosses the president's desk it is most likely destined for a veto. Others believe it is because congressmen don't want to "rock the boat." They know that when they are out of office, they will have a good chance of getting a high paying lobbying job providing they played the game properly. Big money interests have control. So, win or lose, they win.

Today, the American people do not believe that the establishment is serving the people or the country.[3] They no longer believe in the election process and that having a choice to participate in such is an illusion. They no longer believe that the establishment is going to solve the problems facing America. Americans are nauseated by politicians who are more interested in extending their cushy jobs than serving the nation. They also believe that there are few (if any) good choices when it comes to electing politicians that represent them.

Ignorance

"If a nation expects to be ignorant and free, in a state of civilization, it expects what never was and never will be." – Thomas Jefferson

Ignorance is defined as the lack of knowledge, whether intentional or unintentional. Worse yet, it is the turning away from the truth.

According to a 2014 UK Ipsos Mori survey of 11,527 people, the United States ranked second only behind Italy as to how little we understand about some of the most basic aspects of our society.[1]

Being able to make informed choices or whether you can even make a choice for that matter is impossible without knowledge. For instance, say you want to put a new floor in one of the rooms of your house. You would want to know what materials are available, cost, delivery charges, labor charges, timing, and the contractor's reputation (including references) before making any choices. Say you wanted to go out for an ice cream, but you didn't know where to go. Without looking up the location of nearby establishments, you could not make a choice.

As basic as the above sounds, it is astonishing to

see how many Americans do not or will not take the time to find out how candidates stand on issues during an election. These are the very people that are going to affect what choices Americans may or may not be able to make in the future. People seem to be more interested in candidates' personalities, tabloid stories about them, what they wear, or what they had for breakfast. It could be said that the above might add to the equation, but let's face it - in today's world, all candidates are cut from the same cloth. If you want to make an informed choice, you must dig much deeper.

Admittedly, getting past the obvious and down to what a candidate stands for and how they would solve issues is not an easy task. Especially, since they are part of the establishment and given the fact that you are not going to get the truth from the media. Many people just don't want to bother and many are drawn into believing that it does not matter anyway. To make it easy, they just go along with the candidate that has an agreeable personality, not investigating any further. Others that have limited knowledge would contend that they are voting for the lessor of two bad choices. Then there are those that just choose to stay away from politics altogether as they have too many other things to worry about.

Historically, young people aged 18 to 29 have expressed less interest in politics, current events and laws.[2] If you fall into this category, you need to understand that those that get into office are probably going to affect your lives more than anyone. One of the best suggestions I can give to become informed, is to start by reading and understanding the Constitution. Dr. Ben Carson's book, *A More Perfect Union* is a terrific place to start.[3]

Additionally, find out how new laws are going to affect your pocketbook and your choices. When a friend or family member says they don't like someone that is running for office, ask them why. Because they don't like the way a candidate looks or they don't like their personality or that they are not qualified are not acceptable answers. Ask them to be more specific and have them provide backup for what they say. If they can't give you reasonable answers, find another source. Take the time to find out for yourself and if what you learn coincides with your beliefs, then can you make an informed choice.

Andrew Jackson once warned, "But you must remember, my fellow citizens, that eternal vigilance by the people is the price of liberty, and that you must pay the price if you wish to secure the blessing. It behooves you, therefore, to be watchful in your States as well as in the Federal Government." Eliminating ignorance in itself is a choice. Dark be the day when we no longer have that choice.

Fed Up

"Yeah, because I'm fed up with that" - Andrew Murray

Informed Americans are not just fed up with the establishment itself. They are also fed up with what is happening in the country as a result of the policies and actions of the establishment and the current administration. They are fed up with divisive policies that pit blacks against whites, women against men, rich against poor, non-taxpayers against taxpayers, and citizens against cops. Informed Americans are fed up with hate groups that feed on divisiveness, causing chaos wherever and whenever they can. These are not like the movements in the 1960s and 1970s. They exist only to further divide the country, not to bring it together.

Informed Americans are fed up with an administration that apologizes for America while refusing to call Islamic terrorists by name.[1] They are fed up with the continuing attack on Christian values and beliefs. They question why we continue to fund foreign wars that cost trillions of dollars from which we gain nothing. They question the reason we spend billions to help other countries in the world to promote democracy while our national debt continues to rise, and at the same time we fail to meet the

125

needs of our hungry and poor.

Informed Americans are disgusted with this nation's fiscal irresponsibility, its ever increasing entitlements and Washington's refusal to reel them in. They are fed up with politically correct bullies. They despise lectures about not paying our fair share when half the income earners don't pay any income taxes.[2] They are fed up with lies about decreasing unemployment rates when millions have dropped out of the workforce.[3]

It seems that every other week, we face a new threat to our nation that the establishment and administration meets with barely disguised indifference. Islamic terrorism is overrunning the Middle East and has reached our mainland and all we hear about is more gun control. The borders are not enforced nor are immigration laws. Amnesty is given to millions of immigrants who are here illegally.[4] Sanctuary cities that harbor criminal immigrants are ignored.

These are just a few of the rants of informed American citizens. So where does this leave us? People have heard too many times that one party or the other will turn things around. Many have quit believing either party will reverse this madness should they acquire full control. So, do we just give up and continue to let those in power dictate how we run our lives? Actually, the choices are very clear. We either continue down the destructive path that we are on or we start to elect and hold accountable people that cherish the Constitution and represent the principles, values, and beliefs of our founding fathers.

Conclusion

The issues contained in the preceding chapters are disturbing and worrisome. It indicates that the very fabric of our nation is quickly fraying and that the future looks uncertain. It lends credence to the fact that we are well on our way down the slippery slope to a socialist state. Those that escaped tyranny and religious persecution to found a new country where freedom and liberty is the rule, rather than the exception, would be appalled at what America has become. They would be horrified at the way our Constitution is being challenged and the way government has grown to rule over just about every choice we make. They would be dismayed by the amount of uninformed citizens. They would be disgusted with the disconnection and dysfunction of all branches of the Federal Government.

In its short history, America has overcome many difficult challenges. The internal ones that we are faced with now arc many and difficult. Meeting these challenges requires strong leaders at all levels of government. That is, leaders who are willing to put the American people first. America needs leaders who promote a positive, cooperative atmosphere among all branches of government. We need to have confidence in leaders that are willing to pass legislation that provides opportunities for the success of all Americans.

We should demand that leaders uphold the Constitution and promote democracy and capitalism.

If we are to remain a free and democratic society, it is of the utmost importance that every person stays informed, questions everything, and participates in their right to vote at every level of government. Learn who your local elected officials are and what they are doing to improve your community. Learn about your State and Federal Representatives, and Senators. Look at their websites and Facebook pages. Look up their voting records. Send them email or post to their sites and tell them how you feel about current issues. Ask questions and hold them accountable for their actions. Tell them this madness has to stop. As hard as it may be to believe, it is still in the hands of the people as long as we have that right.

It would seem that all the negative stuff that trickles down from the federal and state governments would settle at the grassroots level. Ironically, just the opposite is true. Charitable and community service organizations, people willing to help out in hard times and during disasters, church organizations, and small town businesses, are doing good work. Wouldn't it be nice if we could find a way to "trickle up" some good and positive things that are going on?

At the beginning, it was asked, "Do the American people still have the capability to make choices based on truth and logic?"

Maybe a better question is, "Do the American people still want to have choices?"

Epilogue

Writing this book provided me with an eye-opening education – one that I plan to continue to pursue. In doing so, I would like to hear from you. In that light, I invite you to join the *Choices* group page on Facebook. The group is open to all and encourages open debate on any subject that affects choices for Americans. To start things off, I have a homework assignment for participants. Google "The North American Union" and determine how you think it would affect your future choices. Hope to see you there.

Notes

Making Informed Choices

1. Mark Rice, 4 December 2013, Ranking America, "The U.S ranks 24th in literacy," 30 October 2014, "The U.S. ranks 2nd in ignorance," 6 January 2015, "The U.S. ranks 14th in education" https://rankingamerica.wordpress.com/category/education/

Is Choice a Freedom?

1. Merriam Webster, "Simple Definition of Choice" http://www.merriam-webster.com/dictionary/choice

How Choices are Manipulated and Restricted

1. Elizabeth Whitman, 21 September 2015, IBT, "Overpaying For Health Insurance? - 2 Million On Obamacare Missing Out On Cost-Cutting Subsidies, Study Finds" http://www.ibtimes.com/overpaying-health-insurance-2-million-obamacare-missing-out-cost-cutting-subsidies-2063546

The Story of a Nation

1. Jerry Rye, 5 August 2015, Youtube, Argentina https://www.youtube.com/watch?v=33i_BAhuiE0

2. Wikipedia – The Free Encyclopedia, "Corporatism" https://en.wikipedia.org/wiki/Corporatism

3. Anglo Info - Argentina, "Value Added Tax (VAT) in Argentina" https://www.angloinfo.com/argentina/how-to/page/argentina-money-general-taxes-value-added-tax

4. Anatoly Kurmanaev and Maolis Castro, 12 February 2016, The Wall Street Journal, "Venezuela's Collapse Brings Savage Suffering" http://www.wsj.com/articles/venezuelas-collapse-brings-savage-suffering-1455323300

5. Kin Weisman, 2 April 2000, Congress Action Newsletter, "Socialism Still A Failure" http://www.tysknews.com/Depts/gov_philosophy/socialism_still_a_failure.htm

Notes

The First and Second Amendments to the Constitution

1. Pamela Geller, 4 April 2014, Pamela Geller, "Dearborn: Muslim parents angry over Easter egg hunt school flyer" http://pamelageller.com/2014/04/muslim-parents-angry-easter-egg-hunt-school-flyer.html/

Political Correctness

1. FoxNews.com, 26 July 2012, Fox News, "Pornography at San Francisco library prompts privacy screens" http://www.foxnews.com/us/2012/07/26/pornography-at-san-francisco-library-reportedly-prompts-privacy-screens.html?test=latestnews

2. Todd Starns, Todd Starns Radio, "School Orders Child to Remove God From Poem" http://radio.foxnews.com/toddstarnes/top-stories/school-orders-child-to-remove-god-from-poem.html

3. Jenny Erikson, 26 March 2013, The Stir, "Refusing to Stomp on Jesus's Name Gets Student Banned From Class" http://thestir.cafemom.com/in_the_news/153187/refusing_to_stomp_on_jesuss

4. Nathan Wold, 25 August 2015, +LISTVERSE, "10 Most Absurd Things Banned On Politically Correct College Campuses" http://listverse.com/2015/08/25/10-most-absurd-things-to-ban-on-politically-correct-college-campuses/

The Media

1. Eugene Volokh, 4 April 2011, The Volokh Conspirasy, ""The Freedom ... of the Press," from 1791 to 1868 to Now — Freedom for the Press as an Industry, or the Press as a Technology?"" http://volokh.com/2011/04/04/%E2%80%9Cthe-freedom-of-the-press%E2%80%9D-from-1791-to-1868-to-now-freedom-for-the-press-as-an-industry-or-the-press-as-a-technology/

2. Paul Farhi, 13 June 2013, Real Clear Politics, "Conflicts Abound w/Ties Between Media & Obama Admin" http://www.realclearpolitics.com/2013/06/13/conflicts_abound_wties_between_media_amp_obama_admin_309674.html

Choices

3. Mark Jurkowitz, 5 June 2013, Pew Research Center, "Is MSNBC the place for opinion?"
http://www.pewresearch.org/fact-tank/2013/06/05/is-msnbc-the-place-for-opinion/

4. Richard Salant Quote, Libertytree.ca
http://quotes.liberty-tree.ca/quote_blog/Richard.Salant.Quote.FE9B

Education

1. IES>NCES -National Center for Educational Statistics, "The National Assessment of Educational Progress"
http://nces.ed.gov/nationsreportcard/

2. 29 June 2015, ATLAS, "Federal, State, and Local K-12 School Finance Overview"
http://atlas.newamerica.org/school-finance

3. Michael Rosenbaum, 26 February 2015, The Hill, "Rewriting history and the pursuit of ignorance"
http://thehill.com/blogs/pundits-blog/education/233911-rewriting-history-and-the-pursuit-of-ignorance

4. Stan Karp, volume 28, No 2 - Winter 2013/14, rethinking Schools, "The Problems with the Common Core"
http://www.rethinkingschools.org/archive/28_02/28_02_karp.shtml

5. The Silencing – How the Left is Killing Free Speech by Kirsten Powers. ISBN 978-1-62157-370-8 (hardback). Published by Regnery Publishing, A Division of Salem Media Group, 300 New Jersey Ave NW, Washington, DC 2001, www.Regnery.com

6. Nicole Hemmer, 3 June 2014, US News, "Conservatives Vanish from Commencement"
http://www.usnews.com/opinion/blogs/nicole-hemmer/2014/06/03/colleges-leave-conservatives-out-of-commencement-ceremonies

7 Nick Gass, 2 May 2016, Politico, "Bloomberg booed as he rips college safe spaces'"
http://www.politico.com/story/2016/05/michael-bloomberg-booed-michigan-commencement-222691

132

8. 19 September 2013, FIRE, "Free Speech Zones on America's Campuses"
https://www.thefire.org/infographic-free-speech-zones-on-americas-campuses-2/

9. Matt Reagan, 11 September 2014, desiring God, "When Your Campus Ministry Is "Derecognized""
http://www.desiringgod.org/articles/when-your-campus-ministry-is-derecognized

10. Mark Kantrowitz, 11 January 2016, Money College Planner, "Why the Student Loan Crisis Is Even Worse Than People Think"
http://time.com/money/4168510/why-student-loan-crisis-is-worse-than-people-think/

11. Collegedata - your online college advisor, "What's the Price Tag for a College Education?"
http://www.collegedata.com/cs/content/content_payarticle_tmpl.jhtml?articleId=10064

Jobs and Wages

1. Heather Long, 29 March 2016, CNN Money, "U.S. has lost 5 million manufacturing jobs since 2000"
http://money.cnn.com/2016/03/29/news/economy/us-manufacturing-jobs/

2 CNBC, 31 July 2012, Huff Post - News and Trends - Small Business, "Is There a High Tech Worker Shortage In The US?"
http://www.huffingtonpost.com/2012/05/31/is-there-a-high-tech-work_n_1559901.html

3. Mark Koba, 29 May 2012, CNBC, "High Tech Worker Shortage: Has Anything Changed?"
http://www.cnbc.com/id/46902840

4. Elise Gould, 19 February 2015, Economic Policy Institute, "2014 Continues a 35-Year Trend of Broad-Based Wage Stagnation"
http://www.epi.org/publication/stagnant-wages-in-2014/

Poverty

1. Carmen DeNavas and Walt and Bernadette D. Proctor, September 2015, "Income and Poverty in the Unite States: 2014"
https://www.census.gov/content/dam/Census/library/publications/2015/demo/p60-252.pdf

2. Robert Rector, 28 September 2015, Hertage.org, "Poverty in the U.S. — We Spend Much More Per Person on Social Welfare than Europe Does"
http://www.heritage.org/research/commentary/2015/9/americas-antipoverty-spending-dwarfs-europe

3. Robert Rector, Solutions 2016, heritage.org, "Welfare"
http://solutions.heritage.org/entitlements/welfare/

4. Michael Tanner & Charles Hughes, 2013, Cato Institute, "The Works vs Welfare Tradoff: 2013"
http://object.cato.org/sites/cato.org/files/pubs/pdf/the_work_versus_welfare_trade-off_2013_wp.pdf

5. Vee Burke, 1 July 2003, royce.house.gov, "The 1996 Welfare Reform Law"
http://royce.house.gov/uploadedfiles/the%201996%20welfare%20reform%20law.pdf

Redistribution of Wealth
1. US Government Spending, "US Entitlement Spending Growth"
http://www.usgovernmentspending.com/entitlement_spending

2. Chris Edwards, 4 April 2016, Down Sizing the Federal Government, "A Plan to Cut Federal Government Spending"
http://www.downsizinggovernment.org/plan-to-cut-federal-spending

3. Scott Rohter, February 2012, Less Gov is Best Gov, "U.S. Government Entitlement Programs - Are They Good or Bad? From Independence to Co-dependents in Just a Few Generations"
http://lessgovisthebestgov.com/US-government-entitlement-programs-good-or-bad.html

4. S. Noble, 10 July 2015, Independant Sentinal, "It's Not If But When the Government Seizes Private Retirement Savings"
https://www.independentsentinel.com/retirement-socialism-usa-government-seizes-private-retirement-savings/

Free Enterprise
1. Lydia Wheeler, 30 December 2015, The Hill, "Study: 2015 was record year for federal regulation"
http://thehill.com/regulation/administration/264456-2015-was-record-year-for-federal-regulation-group-says

Notes

2. Clyde Wayne Crews, 8 May 2015, Competive Enterprise Institute, "Ten Thousand Commandments 2015 - An Annual Snapshot of the Federal Regulatory State"
https://cei.org/10kc2015

Competition
1. July 2002, New Internationalists Magazine, "A Short History Of Corporations"
http://newint.org/features/2002/07/05/history/

2. Melissa Block, 24 Oct 2011, NPR, "What Is The Basis For Corporate Personhood?"
http://www.npr.org/2011/10/24/141663195/what-is-the-basis-for-corporate-personhood

3. Lee Drutman, 20 April 2015, The Atlantic, "How Corporate Lobbyists Conquered American Democracy"
http://www.theatlantic.com/business/archive/2015/04/how-corporate-lobbyists-conquered-american-democracy/390822/

4. Infoplease, "Sherman Antitrust Act"
http://www.infoplease.com/encyclopedia/history/sherman-antitrust-act.html

5. John W. Whitehead, 8 September 2012, Huffpost Politics, "The Corporate Takeover of America — A Government of the Elites, by the Bureaucrats and for the Corporations"
http://www.huffingtonpost.com/john-w-whitehead/national-governors-association_b_1658805.html

6. J.D. Harrison, 12 February 2016, The Washington Post, "The decline of American entrepreneurship — in five charts"
https://www.washingtonpost.com/news/on-small-business/wp/2015/02/12/the-decline-of-american-entrepreneurship-in-five-charts/

Trade
1,2. Frank William Taussig, 1931, "The tariff history of the United States"
https://archive.org/details/tariffhistoryun02tausgoog

3. Wikipedia, "Comparative advantage"
https://en.wikipedia.org/wiki/Comparative_advantage

4. AFP, 5 February 2016, Yahoo News, "US trade deficit grows in 2015 as exports weaken"
https://www.yahoo.com/news/us-trade-deficit-grows-2015-exports-weaken-135439974.html?ref=gs

5. 8 June 2015, The Wall Street Journal, "Trade Deficit Myths - A case study in protectionist misinformation"
http://www.wsj.com/articles/trade-deficit-myths-1433804035

6. Robert E. Scott, 13 January 2016, The Economic Institute, "Trans-Pacific Partnership AgreementCurrency manipulation, trade, wages, and job loss"
http://www.epi.org/publication/trans-pacific-partnership-agreement-currency-manipulation-trade-wages-and-job-loss/

The Food Supply

1,2. June 2014, PUBLICCITIZEN, "Food Imports to the United States Soar under WTO-NAFTA Model, Threatening American Farmers and Safety"
https://www.citizen.org/documents/food-under-nafta-wto.pdf

3. Kimberly Amadeo, 8 February 2016, About Money, "Why Are Food Prices Rising? Causes of Food Price Inflation"
http://useconomy.about.com/od/inflationfaq/f/Why-Are-Food-Prices-So-High.htm

4. Dr. Mercola, 23 September 2013, Mercola.com, "Is There Really a Problem with Food Shortages in the US?"
http://articles.mercola.com/sites/articles/archive/2015/09/23/food-shortage-security.aspx

5. March 2011, fightbac.org, "Emerging Issues"
http://www.fightbac.org/wp-content/uploads/2015/08/Emerging_Food_Safety_Issues_White_Paper.pdf

6. Andrew Bosworth, 22 October 2008, UNDERNEWS, "Forcing Terminator Seeds on Iraq"
http://www.prorev.com/2008/10/forcing-terminator-seeds-on-iraq.html

7. Sara Morrison, 23 February 2013, Independant, "Too much power in too few hands: Food giants take over the industry"
http://www.independent.co.uk/life-style/food-and-drink/news/too-much-power-in-too-few-hands-food-giants-take-over-the-industry-8508259.html#disqus_thread

8. 28 August 2015, The Daily Sheeple, "Why Did Obama Nationalize the U.S. Food Supply with Executive Order 13603?" http://www.thedailysheeple.com/why-did-obama-nationalize-the-u-s-food-supply-with-executive-order-13603_082015

Safety and Security

1. Wikipedia, "H.R. 5122 (2006)" https://en.wikipedia.org/wiki/H.R._5122_%282006%29

2. ACLU, 31 December 2011, "President Obama Signs Indefinite Detention Bill Into Law" https://www.aclu.org/news/president-obama-signs-indefinite-detention-bill-law

3. Robert Richardson, Offgrid Survival, "Martial Law in the United States: How Likely is it, and What will happen under Martial law?" http://offgridsurvival.com/martiallaw-unitedstates/

4. Kim M., 28 October 2013, InfoWars, "20 Drills that Prove the DHS' Official New Enemy is the American People" http://www.infowars.com/20-urban-shield-2013-scenarios-which-prove-the-terrorists-are-us/

5. Jesse Hathaway, 10 February 2014, Mediatrackers, "Ohio National Guard Training Envisions Right-Wing Terrorism" http://mediatrackers.org/ohio/2014/02/10/ohio-national-guard-training-envisions-right-wing-terrorism

6. Dan Lamothe, 14 September 2014, The Washington Post, "Remember Jade Helm 15, the controversial military exercise? It's over." https://www.washingtonpost.com/news/checkpoint/wp/2015/09/14/remember-jade-helm-15-the-controversial-military-exercise-its-over/

Illegal Immigration

1. FAIR - Federation for American Immigration Reform, "Immigration Facts" http://www.fairus.org/facts

2. Guest Opinion, 29 October 2014, Immigration Reform, "Illegal immigrants send home $50 billion annually but cost taxpayers more than $113 billion"
http://immigrationreform.com/2014/10/29/illegal-immigrants-send-home-50-billion-annually-but-cost-taxpayers-more-than-113-billion/

3. Simon Tomlinson, 31 January 2013, Daily Mail, "Revealed: How immigrants in America are sending $120 BILLION to their struggling families back home"
http://www.dailymail.co.uk/news/article-2271455/Revealed-How-immigrants-America-sending-120-BILLION-struggling-families-home.html

4. Joel Gehrke, 28 July 2015, Nation Review, "Report: U.S. Spent $1.87 Billion to Incarcerate Illegal-Immigrant Criminals in 2014"
http://www.nationalreview.com/article/421673/nearly-2-billion-spent-jailing-illegal-immigrant-criminals-america-2014

5. Jessica Vaughan, November 2009, Center for Immigration Studies, "Immigration and Crime: Assessing a Conflicted Issue"
http://cis.org/ImmigrantCrime

6. BJA - Bureau of Justice Assistance - U.S. Department of Justice, "State Criminal Alien Assistance Program (SCAAP)"
https://www.bja.gov/ProgramDetails.aspx?Program_ID=86

7. GAO - United States Government Accountability Office, March 2011, "Report to Congressional Requesters - CRIMINAL ALIEN STATISTICS - Information on Incarcerations, Arrests, and Costs"
http://www.gao.gov/assets/320/316959.pdf

8. ICE - U.S. Immigration and Customs Enforcement, "FY 2015 ICE Immigration Removals"
https://www.ice.gov/removal-statistics

9. WND, 25 October 2015, "Astonishing' crime stats for illegal aliens"
http://www.wnd.com/2015/10/astonishing-crime-stats-for-illegal-aliens/

10. FBI - Federal Bureau of Investigation, "2011 National Gang Threat Assessment – Emerging Trends"
https://www.fbi.gov/stats-services/publications/2011-national-gang-threat-assessment

Notes

11. Alistair Bell, 7 August 2014, Reuters, "Americans worry that illegal migrants threaten way of life, economy"
http://www.reuters.com/article/us-usa-immigration-worries-idUSKBN0G70BE20140807

Refugees

1. Immigration to North America, "World War II and immigration Records"
http://immigrationtous.net/319-world-war-ii-and-immigration.html

2. PUBLIC LAW 96-212, 17 March 1980
https://www.gpo.gov/fdsys/pkg/STATUTE-94/pdf/STATUTE-94-Pg102.pdf

3. Amy Pope, 20 November 2015, whitehouse.gov, "Infographic: The Screening Process for Refugee Entry into the United States"
https://www.whitehouse.gov/blog/2015/11/20/infographic-screening-process-refugee-entry-united-states

4. The White House - Office of the Press Secretary, 21 November 2014, whitehouse.gov, "Presidential Memorandum -- Creating Welcoming Communities and Fully Integrating Immigrants and Refugees"
https://www.whitehouse.gov/the-press-office/2014/11/21/presidential-memorandum-creating-welcoming-communities-and-fully-integra

5. Teresa Lynn, 13 May 2015, The Realside, "Were fast tracking 600,00 Islamic Syrian refugees to citizenship. Are you ready?"
http://therealside.com/2015/05/were-fast-tracking-600000-islamic-syrian-refugees-to-citizenship-are-you-ready/

6. Chuck Ross, 21 October 2015, The Daily Craller, "FBI Director Admits US Can't Vet All Syrian Refugees For Terror Ties"
http://dailycaller.com/2015/10/21/fbi-director-admits-us-cant-vet-all-syrian-refugees-for-terror-ties-video/

7. U.S immigration legislation online, 27 June 1952, "1952 Immigration and Nationality Act, a.k.a. the McCarran-Walter Act"
http://library.uwb.edu/static/USimmigration/1952_immigration_and_nationality_act.html

8. Caroline May, 16 November 2015, Breitbart, "Sen. Jeff
Sessions: No 'Blank Check' For Syrian Refugees Amid Nat'l
Security Concerns, High Price Tag"
http://www.breitbart.com/big-government/2015/11/16/sen-jeff-
sessions-no-blank-check-syrian-refugees-amid-natl-security-
concerns-high-price-tag/

Paternalism

1. Matt Agorist, 15 April 2016, The Free Thought Project.com,
"Nanny State Run Amok — Cops Now Arresting Parents for
Walking Children Home From School"
http://thefreethoughtproject.com/nanny-state-run-amok-cops-
arresting-parents-walking-children-home-school/

2. MR Conservative, "19 Signs That America Has Become A Nanny
State"
https://www.mrconservative.com/2012/02/2392-american-
control-freaks/

Crime

1. FBI – 2015 January – June, "Crime in the United States"
https://www.fbi.gov/about-us/cjis/ucr/crime-in-the-
u.s/2015/preliminary-semiannual-uniform-crime-report-
januaryjune-2015/tables/table-1

2. Alexander Trowbridge, 1 July 2014, CBS News, "Identity theft
rises, consumers rage"
http://www.cbsnews.com/news/identity-theft-rises-consumers-
rage/

3. Federal Trade Commission, Consumer Information, "Privacy
Choices for Your Personal Financial Information"
https://www.consumer.ftc.gov/articles/0222-privacy-choices-
your-personal-financial-information

Drugs

1. NIH, National Institute on Drug Abuse, June 2015, "DrugFacts:
Nationwide Trends"
https://www.drugabuse.gov/publications/drugfacts/nationwide-
trends

2. NCAAD, National Council on Alcohol and Drug Dependance, 26
April 2015, "Facts about Drugs"
https://www.ncadd.org/about-addiction/faq/facts-about-drugs

Notes

3..DEA Intelligence Report, April 2015, "National Heroin Threat Assessment Summary"
http://www.dea.gov/divisions/hq/2015/hq052215_National_Hero in_Threat_Assessment_Summary.pdf

4. Bill OReilly, 21 July 2015 , Real Clear Politics, "Obama Commutes "Non Violent" Offenders; Bill O'Reilly: "Selling Drugs Is A Violent Crime"
http://www.realclearpolitics.com/video/2015/07/21/obama_com mutes_non_violent_offenders_bill_oreilly_selling_drugs_is_a_violent _crime.html

5. Talbott Recovery, "2015 Prescription Drug Abuse Statistics You Need to Know"
https://talbottcampus.com/index.php/resources/disease-info/2015-prescription-drug-abuse-statistics/

6. John Keilman, 24 March 2016, Chicago Tribune, "Almost all doctors routinely overprescribe pain pills: survey"
http://www.chicagotribune.com/news/local/breaking/ct-prescription-painkiller-overuse-met-20160324-story.html

7. Lynn Arditi, 22 May 2015, Providence Journal, "DEA report: Heroin use growing faster than any other illicit drug; overdose deaths highest in a decade"
http://www.providencejournal.com/article/20150522/NEWS/150 529638

8. NIH, National Institute on Drug Abuse, December 2015, "Overdose Death Rates"
https://www.drugabuse.gov/related-topics/trends-statistics/overdose-death-rates

The Grievance Industry

1. Ashe Schow, 30 March 2016, The Washington Examiner, "The cottage industry of campus grievance culture"
http://www.washingtonexaminer.com/the-cottage-industry-of-campus-grievance-culture/article/2587195

2. Rob Walsh, 3 May 2013, Library Journal, "Fringe Politics: Hate and Extremism | Collection Development"
http://reviews.libraryjournal.com/2013/05/collection-development/fringe-politics-hate-and-extremism/

Choices

3. Niraj Chokshi, 17 February 2016, The Washington Post, "The year of 'enormous rage': Number of hate groups rose by 14 percent in 2015"
https://www.washingtonpost.com/news/acts-of-faith/wp/2016/02/17/hate-groups-rose-14-percent-last-year-the-first-increase-since-2010/

Big Government
1. David Boaz, 1 April 1997, FEE – Foundation for Economic Education, "What Big Government Is All About"
https://fee.org/articles/what-big-government-is-all-about/

2. Federal Register – The Daily Journal of the United States
https://www.federalregister.gov/agencies

3. Terence P. Jeffrey, 8 September 2015, CNS News, "21,995,000 to12,329,000: Government Employees Outnumber Manufacturing Employees 1.8 to 1"
http://cnsnews.com/news/article/terence-p-jeffrey/21955000-12329000-government-employees-outnumber-manufacturing

Debt
1. Dave Boyer, 1 November 2015, The Washington Times, "$20 trillion man: National debt nearly doubles during Obama presidency"
http://www.washingtontimes.com/news/2015/nov/1/obama-presidency-to-end-with-20-trillion-national-/?page=all

2. Dave Manual, davemanual.com,"A History of Surpluses and Deficits in the United States"
http://www.davemanuel.com/history-of-deficits-and-surpluses-in-the-united-states.php

3. Treasury Direct, 5 May 2013, "Historical Debt Outstanding - Annual 1950 – 1999"
https://www.treasurydirect.gov/govt/reports/pd/histdebt/histdebt_histo4.htm

4. Staff wire reports, 28 June 1999, CNN Money, "Clinton: Pay debt by 2015"
http://money.cnn.com/1999/06/28/economy/clinton/

5. GAO - United States Government Accountability Office, November 2015 Report to the Secretary of Treasury, "FINANCIAL AUDIT - Bureau of the Fiscal Service's Fiscal Years 2015 and 2014 Schedules of Federal Debt"
https://www.treasurydirect.gov/govt/reports/pd/feddebt/feddebt_ann2015.pdf

6. Thomas Kenny, About Money, "What is the European Debt Crisis?
http://bonds.about.com/od/advancedbonds/a/What-Is-The-European-Debt-Crisis.htm

7. Center on Budget and Policy Priorities, 12 February 2016, "Policy Basics: Deficits, Debt, and Interest"
http://www.cbpp.org/research/federal-budget/policy-basics-deficits-debt-and-interest

8. Social Security – Official Social Security Website, "Frequently Asked Questions about the Social Security Trust Funds"
https://www.ssa.gov/oact/progdata/fundFAQ.html#&a0=3

9. Dr. Allen Smith, 19 July 2011, Sott – Sign of the Times, "Social Security Scam: Where did the $2.5 Trillion Surplus Go?"
https://www.sott.net/article/232087-Social-Security-Scam-Where-Did-the-2-5-Trillion-Surplus-Go

10,12,14,15. US Debt Clock.org
http://www.usdebtclock.org/

11. Richard W. Rahn, 16 February 2015. The Washington Times, "The world's greatest financial fraudster - How the U.S. government wastes $1 trillion every year"
http://www.washingtontimes.com/news/2015/feb/16/richard-rahn-us-government-wastes-1-trillion-a-yea/

13. Investors World, "unfunded liability"
http://www.investorwords.com/19346/unfunded_liability.html

The Federal Reserve

1. Board of Governers of the Federal Reserve System, "What is the purpose of the Federal Reserve System?"
https://www.federalreserve.gov/faqs/about_12594.htm

2. The Federal Reserve Board, "The Twelve Federal Reserve Districts"
http://www.federalreserve.gov/otherfrb.htm

3. David Dayen, 9 March 2014, New Republic, "This Is the Fed's Most Brazen and Least Known Handout to Private Banks" https://newrepublic.com/article/116913/federal-reserve-dividends-most-outrageous-handout-banks

4. Kimberly Amadeo, 21 April 2016, About Money, "Who Owns the U.S. National Debt? - The Biggest Owner Is You!" http://useconomy.about.com/od/monetarypolicy/f/Who-Owns-US-National-Debt.htm

5. 5. John Aziz, 30 May 2013, The Week, "Does the Federal Reserve really control the money supply?" http://theweek.com/articles/463787/does-federal-reserve-really-control-money-supply

6. Jordain Carney, 12 January 2016, The Hill, "Senate rejects Paul's push to audit the Fed" http://thehill.com/blogs/floor-action/senate/265589-senate-rejects-pauls-audit-the-fed-push

The Economy

1. David Kupelian, 19 March 2008, WND, "Bernanke: Federal Reserve caused Great Depression" http://www.wnd.com/2008/03/59405/

2. Washington University in St. Louis, Muddy Water Macro, "Causes of the Great Recession" https://muddywatermacro.wustl.edu/node/92

3. The State of Working America, Economic Policy Institute, "The Great Recession" http://stateofworkingamerica.org/great-recession/

4. U.S. Department of Commerce, Bureau of Economic Analysis, "U.S. Economy at a Glance: Perspective from the BEA Accounts" http://www.bea.gov/newsreleases/glance.htm

5. Kinberly Amadeo, 4 April 2016, About Money, "What Is the Ideal GDP Growth Rate?" http://useconomy.about.com/od/grossdomesticproduct/f/Ideal_GDP.htm

Notes

6. Center on budget and Policy Priorities, 10 May 2016, "Chart Book: The Legacy of the Great Recession" http://www.cbpp.org/research/economy/chart-book-the-legacy-of-the-great-recession

Taxes

1. Tyler Durden, 15 April 2013, 0Zero Hedge, "100 Years Old & Still Killing Us: America Was Much Better Off Before The Income Tax" http://www.zerohedge.com/news/2013-04-15/100-years-old-still-killing-us-america-was-much-better-income-tax

2. Drew Desilver, 13 April 2016, Pew Research Center, "High-income Americans pay most income taxes, but enough to be 'fair" http://www.pewresearch.org/fact-tank/2016/04/13/high-income-americans-pay-most-income-taxes-but-enough-to-be-fair/

3. Louis Jacobson, 18 April, 2011, Politifact, "Michele Bachmann says top 1 percent pay 40 percent of all federal taxes" http://www.politifact.com/truth-o-meter/statements/2011/apr/18/michele-bachmann/michele-bachmann-says-top-1-percent-pay-40-percent/

4. Michael Snyder, 6 December 2012, The Economic Collapse, "Show This To Anyone That Believes That Taxes Are Too Low" http://theeconomiccollapseblog.com/archives/show-this-to-anyone-that-believes-that-taxes-are-too-low

5. Obamacare Facts, "Supreme Court ObamaCare | Ruling on ObamaCare" http://obamacarefacts.com/supreme-court-obamacare/

6,7. Derek Tsang, 9 September 2014, Punditfact, "Does the U.S. have the highest corporate tax rate in the free world?" http://www.politifact.com/punditfact/statements/2014/sep/09/eric-bolling/does-us-have-highest-corporate-tax-rate-free-world/

8. Thomas L. Hungerford, 8 September 2014, Economic Policy Institute, "Policy Responses to Corporate Inversions" http://www.epi.org/publication/policy-responses-corporate-inversions/

9. Zachary Mider, Jesse Drucker, 6 April 2016, Bloomber Quicktake, "Tax Inversion How U.S. Companies Buy Tax Breaks" http://www.bloombergview.com/quicktake/tax-inversion

145

10. Kyle Pomerleau, 14 August 2014, Tax Foundation, "How Much Will Corporate Tax Inversions Cost the U.S. Treasury?" http://taxfoundation.org/blog/how-much-will-corporate-tax-inversions-cost-us-treasury

Health Care

1. AMA - American Medical Association, "Our History" http://www.ama-assn.org/ama/pub/about-ama/our-history.page?

2. Social Security - Legislative History, "The Social Security Act of 1935" https://www.ssa.gov/history/law.html

3. Harry S. Truman, "This Day in Truman History, November 19, 1945, President Truman's Proposed Health Program" http://www.trumanlibrary.org/anniversaries/healthprogram.htm

4. liveOnNY, Transplantation, "Organ Transplant History" http://liveonny.org/all-about-transplantation/organ-transplant-history/

5. The World Bank, "Health expenditure, total (% of GDP)" http://data.worldbank.org/indicator/SH.XPD.TOTL.ZS/countries?page=1

6. Wikipedia, "Donald Berwick" https://en.wikipedia.org/wiki/Donald_Berwick

7. Lori Robertson, 11 April 2014, FactCheck.org, "'Millions' Lost Insurance" http://www.factcheck.org/2014/04/millions-lost-insurance/

8..Betsy McCaughey, 14 January 2014, New York Post, "Another 25 million Obamacare victims" http://nypost.com/2014/01/14/another-25-million-obamacare-victims/

9. Eryn Taylor and TMW via Graphiq, 12 May 2016, News3 - Memphis Tenn, "Why are 29M Americans still living without health insurance?" http://wreg.com/2016/05/12/why-are-29m-americans-still-living-without-health-insurance/

Notes

10. Chriss W. Street, 6 July 2015, breitbart.com, "Ouch! Massive Obamacare Premium Increases Will Dominate 2016"
http://www.breitbart.com/big-government/2015/07/06/ouch-massive-obamacare-premium-increases-will-dominate-2016/

Presidential Elections

1. Tim Hains, 12 April 2016, Real Clear Politics, "Napolitano to Trump: Republican & Democrat Parties Are Private Clubs, "They Are Not Part Of The Government""
http://www.realclearpolitics.com/video/2016/04/12/judge_napol itano_republican_and_democrat_parties_are_private_clubs_not_par t_of_the_government.html

2. Jonathan Masters and Gopal Ratnam, 9 February 2016, Council on Foreign Relations, "The U.S. Presidential Nominating Process"
http://www.cfr.org/elections/us-presidential-nominating-process/p37522

3. Sean Bryant, Investopedia, "How Much Will it Cost to Become President In 2016?"
http://www.investopedia.com/articles/personal-finance/111815/how-much-will-it-cost-become-president-2016.asp

4. John Frank, 25 September 2015, The Denver Post, "Colorado Republicans cancel presidential vote at 2016 caucus"
http://www.denverpost.com/news/ci_28700919/colorado-republicans-cancel-2016-presidential-caucus-vote

5 Martin Gilens and Benjamin I. Page, 18 September 2014, Perspectives on Politics, "Testing Theories of American Politics: Elites, Interest Groups, and Average Citizens"
http://journals.cambridge.org/action/displayAbstract?fromPage= online&aid=9354310&fileId=S1537592714001595

6. Opensecrets.org, "What is a PAC?"
https://www.opensecrets.org/pacs/pacfaq.php

7 Federal Election Commission, 26 March 2010, "Speechnow.org v. FECKeating v. FEC Case Summary"
http://www.fec.gov/law/litigation/speechnow.shtml

8. Opensecrets.org, "Super PACs"
https://www.opensecrets.org/pacs/superpacs.php

9. Opensecrets.org, "Political Nonprofits (Dark Money)"
https://www.opensecrets.org/outsidespending/nonprof_summ.php

10. Opensecrets.org, "Lobbying Database"
http://www.opensecrets.org/lobby/

11. Elizabeth Brown, 18 January 2006, The Center for Public Integrity, "Lobbying FAQ - What is permissible? Out of bounds? Punishable?"
https://www.publicintegrity.org/2006/01/18/6546/lobbying-faq

12. Opensecrets.org, "2016 Campaign Contribution Limits"
http://www.opensecrets.org/overview/limits.php

13. Wikipedia, "Spin Doctors"
https://en.wikipedia.org/wiki/Spin_Doctors

14. 8 November 2012, Bipartisan Policy Center, "2012 Voter Turnout Report"
http://bipartisanpolicy.org/library/2012-voter-turnout/

The Establishment

1. David Lightman, 24 March 2016, McClatchy DC, "America to Establishment: Who the hell are you people?"
http://www.mcclatchydc.com/news/politics-government/election/article68042192.html

2. Chris Cillizza, 3 February 2014, The Washington Post, "How Congress became the most polarized and unproductive it's ever been"
https://www.washingtonpost.com/news/the-fix/wp/2014/02/03/how-congress-became-the-most-polarized-and-unproductive-its-ever-been/

3. Nathaniel Ward, June, 2012, The Heritage Foundation, "Harry Reid's Senate Stifles Debate and Undermines Founders' Vision"
https://www.myheritage.org/news/harry-reids-senate-stifles-debate-and-undermines-founders-vision/#comments

4. Bonnie Kristian, 5 January 2016, RARE Americas's news feed, "Presidents aren't supposed to just act anytime Congress doesn't agree with their desires"
http://rare.us/story/presidents-arent-supposed-to-just-act-anytime-congress-doesnt-agree-with-their-desires/

Notes

Ignorance

1. Fareed Zakara, 11 November 2014, CNN, "Why the Ignorance Index matters"
http://globalpublicsquare.blogs.cnn.com/2014/11/11/why-the-ignorance-index-matters/

2. Amy Mitchell, Jeffrey Gottfried and Katerina Eva Matsa, 1 June 2015, PEW Research Center, "Political Interest and Awareness Lower Among Millennials"
http://www.journalism.org/2015/06/01/political-interest-and-awareness-lower-among-millennials/

3. *A More Perfect Union,* Dr. Ben Carson, ISBN 978-1 59184-2, Published by SENTINEL An imprint of Penguin Random House LLC, 375 Hudson Street, New York, New York, 10014, penguin.com

Fed Up

1. Angie Drobnic Holan, 15 March 2010, "Obama's remarks never a true 'apology'"
http://www.politifact.com/truth-o-meter/obama-quotes/

2. Constitutional Conservatism - A Return to Sanity, "Myth – The Rich Don't Pay Their Fair Share"
https://constitutionalconservative.wordpress.com/myth-the-rich-dont-pay-their-fair-share/

3. Edward Lazear, 6 November 2015, The Washington Post, "This is the real unemployment rate"
https://www.washingtonpost.com/news/wonk/wp/2015/11/06/ed-lazear-this-is-the-real-unemployment-rate/

4. NumbersAmerica – for lower immigration levels, 25 February 2015, "The Seven Amnesties Passed by Congress"
https://www.numbersusa.com/content/learn/illegal-immigration/seven-amnesties-passed-congress.html

Choices

Also by Ron Celano

Create Realistic Portraits with Colored Pencils

Triangulate Your Golf Swing

Golf: A Beginners Guide and Reference

Moving Beyond the Third Fret

Henrietta's Journal

Aunt Bobbie's Favorite Family Recipes

Available at Amazon.com and other online bookstores.